THE NEW
GETTYSBURG
CAMPAIGN
HANDBOOK

JUNE 9 - JULY 14, 1863
FACTS, PHOTOS, AND ARTWORK FOR
READERS OF ALL AGES

Gettysburg PA

J. DAVID PETRUZZI AND STEVEN STANLEY

(Authors of *The Complete Gettysburg Guide* and
The Gettysburg Campaign in Numbers and Losses)

July 30, 2011

SB
Savas Beatie
New York and California

Cataloging-in-Publication Data is available from the Library of Congress.

ISBN 978-1-61121-078-1

05 04 03 02 01   5 4 3 2 1
First edition, first printing

SB

Published by
Savas Beatie LLC
521 Fifth Avenue, Suite 3400
New York, NY 10175

Editorial Offices:

Savas Beatie LLC
P.O. Box 4527
El Dorado Hills, CA 95762
Phone: 916-941-6896
(E-mail) sales@savasbeatie.com

Savas Beatie titles are available at special discounts for bulk purchases worldwide
by corporations, government agencies, institutions, and other organizations.
For more details, please contact Special Sales, P.O. Box 4527, El Dorado Hills, CA
95762, or you may e-mail us at sales@savasbeatie.com, or visit our website at
www.savasbeatie.com for additional information.

Table of Contents

Cover image: *The Battle of Gettysburg* by Paul Philippoteaux (c1883) courtesy of the National Park Service.

Page background: The paper image used for the page background in this book was created from high resolution scans of Jedediah Hotchkiss's Virginia map book courtesy of the Library of Congress.

Photo credits: Unless otherwise noted, all photos are courtesy of Steven Stanley.

Foreword

GETTYSBURG

Almost everyone in the Western world who hears that single word thinks about the American Civil War and the titanic battle that raged for three days. Many may not know where or even exactly when the battle was fought or even who won, but most appreciate the fact that the fighting was important to the outcome of the war.

The battle, fought on July 1-3, 1863, was part of a wide-ranging six-week campaign that included a score of engagements large and small. The defeat of Gen. Robert E. Lee's Army of Northern Virginia was a significant blow to the fortunes of the Confederacy. Unfortunately for the South, the bloody defeat was accompanied on July 4 by the fall of the Confederate fortress and its defending army at Vicksburg, Mississippi, and the surrender of yet another army and stronghold a short time later at Port Hudson, Louisiana. These stunning Western Theater victories opened the final stretch of the Mississippi River to Federal forces and effectively sliced the Confederacy in two. Vicksburg and Port Hudson were preceded by the nearly bloodless Union capture of Middle Tennessee that June when a Federal army maneuvered its Confederate counterpart all the way south to the Georgia border. Because of these nearly simultaneous losses, Gettysburg has led many historians to conclude that the summer of 1863 was a major turning point in the entire war.

Gettysburg has been the focus of intense study and interest since the guns fell silent in 1863. The interest is certainly justified because the campaign has so many fascinating facets to study, ponder, and argue: the most successful

Confederate army commander (Robert E. Lee), engaged in his grandest movement of the war, challenged by the thus-far luckless Army of the Potomac; three bloody days of battle involving all three branches (infantry, artillery, and cavalry); innumerable key moments on all three days upon which teetered victory or defeat; major controversies (including Dan Sickles' movement of his Federal III Corps to the famous Peach Orchard, Jeb Stuart's audacious cavalry ride around the Union army, and Richard Ewell's July 1 failure to capture Cemetery Hill and/or Culp's Hill); thousands of firsthand accounts of nearly every aspect of the fighting; the largest artillery duel ever waged in the Western world; a heart-pounding retreat and pursuit following the battle—and so much more.

When Ted Savas, our publishing company's managing director, approached us with the idea for this handbook and explained what he envisioned, our first reaction was to wonder why no one else had thought of producing such a work. To the best of our knowledge a book like this—with its varied stories, facts, statistics, photos, illustrations, original maps, and so much more—did not exist. Herein, a reader can find out what the weather was like in Gettysburg during the battle, read about the Gettysburg Medal of Honor recipients, discover capsule biographies of the primary leaders, explore an itinerary of the campaign, ponder many of the campaign's controversies, digest a recommended reading list—and even ascertain the various Gettysburg sites available online—all between one set of covers. This book also features the most complete, accurate, and up-to-date Order of Battle for all units of both sides at the Battle of Gettysburg.

Because of the format and purpose of this volume, we acted primarily as compilers and secondarily as authors. We are first and foremost in debt to the legion of participants, scholars, students, and amateur sleuths who recorded the material that has allowed us to bring it to light in one useful resource. Many of the works we relied upon are listed in the chapter entitled "The Gettysburg Bookshelf." (We recommend this list as a good starting point for readers new to the study of this campaign.)

We hope *The New Gettysburg Campaign Handbook* will be a ready and welcome companion whether you are walking the hallowed fields or reading other Gettysburg books while reclining in your favorite easy chair. We hope teachers, parents, students, and scholars will refer to its narratives, photographs, maps, lists, orders of battle, and charts and tables time and time again. It is our sincere wish that this original presentation of the war's greatest campaign adds something of significant value to the voluminous reference shelf of the campaign—especially as we enter the war's sesquicentennial (the commemoration of the 150th anniversary of the Civil War). Finally, we hope this new book will encourage people, young and old alike, to read about this always fascinating portion of our painful history as a country, and plant the seed of interest deeply within them for the rest of their lives.

Acknowledgements

The first book we did together was *The Complete Gettysburg Guide* (Savas Beatie, 2009), an enjoyable project that convinced us how much fun it was to have carte blanche to craft a full color book with dozens of detailed maps, illustrations, and tours. Therefore, when our publisher approached us with this title, we jumped at the opportunity to do it again in a different way. We both owe a debt that can never be repaid to the many Gettysburg Licensed Guides, park rangers, scholars, and friends who have taught us so much over the years about Gettysburg and the campaign. Their personal tours and talks, coupled with their own published and unpublished works, are found in some form or another on nearly every page.

Phil Laino is the cartographer for *The Gettysburg Magazine* and author/ cartographer of the indispensable *Gettysburg Campaign Atlas* (Gatehouse Press, 2009). Phil and his order of battle compiler, **Dr. Steve Floyd**, graciously and generously held a roundhouse email discussion with us for several days as we worked out the Gettysburg Order of Battle you find in this title. Likewise, my good friend **Eric J. Wittenberg**, with whom I have written two previous books—*Plenty of Blame to Go Around: Jeb Stuart's Controversial Ride to Gettysburg* (Savas Beatie, 2006), and, with **Michael Nugent**, *One Continuous Fight: The Retreat from Gettysburg and the Pursuit of Lee's Army of Northern Virginia, July 4-14, 1863* (Savas Beatie, 2008), was of great assistance in developing the orders of battle for several of the other combats of the campaign.

Theodore P. Savas of Savas Beatie has become a creative partner over the years. He is a true friend who offers guidance, motivation, and sage advice while giving us the latitude we desire to frame each project. We hope we have lived up to that trust. The amazing work by the rest of the Savas Beatie marketing team—marketing director **Sarah Keeney**, **Veronica Kane**, **Kim Rouse**, and **Helene Dodier**—keeps us motivated and inspired.

Finally, we want to thank our significant others.

My patient and understanding wife **Karen** deserves the most appreciation of all. She gives up so much of our time together so I can research and write. I'll make it up to you, Karen, I promise—right after I finish that next book . . . Thank you, my dear, for sharing the magic of life with me.

J. David Petruzzi, Brockway, Pennsylvania

This book has impacted my personal life (as all worthwhile books do), but there are two women who stood by me, supported and encouraged me, even though I could not spend as much quality time with them as I should have. Thank you both, **Kyrstie** and **Leigh Ann** for being there for me and understanding, and as J.D. said to Karen, I'll make it up to you both right after that next book.

Steve Stanley, Gettysburg, Pennsylvania

Steven Stanley (left) and J. David Petruzzi (right) perched
in the cupola of the Lutheran Theological Seminary.

Interesting Facts, Figures, and Statistics about the Gettysburg Campaign and Battle

The Gettysburg Campaign, like other conflicts and campaigns of the Civil War, contains its share of interesting facts and statistics. This section contains examples such as the positions of the units of both armies on June 30, 1863 (the day before the battle); weather observations during the battle; and trivia about the campaign and some of its participants.

The study of these interesting facts can enhance our understanding of what took place during the campaign. For instance, what was the weather like during Pickett's Charge? The answer helps us to understand even more of what the soldiers experienced that afternoon. Just as the battle was beginning, how far away were the units of the two armies? Those answers assist us in understanding why particular units arrived on the field at different times.

As the reader explores other books and narratives about the battle and campaign, it is hoped that this section will help to provide a more complete understanding of the atmosphere in which the Battle of Gettysburg took place.

Where Were They?

Following are the general positions of the principal units of each army on June 30, the evening before the Battle of Gettysburg. Please note that due to detachments of, for instance, particular regiments of some brigades, etc., not all units of the following commands were necessarily at each designated location. See the Orders of Battle in this book for details regarding detached commands and units. The mileages to the battlefield are approximate, and are based on the estimated mileage each command would have to march (using roads of the shortest distance) to reach the boundary of the battlefield closest to their June 30 position.

FEDERAL FORCES
ARMY OF THE POTOMAC HEADQUARTERS
Maj. Gen. George G. Meade

Taneytown, Maryland

Distance to Battlefield – 14 miles

First Corps	**Fifth Corps**
Maj. Gen. John F. Reynolds	Maj. Gen. George Sykes
Marsh Run, Maryland	Union Mills, Maryland
Distance to Battlefield – 6 miles	Distance to Battlefield – 14 miles
Second Corps	**Sixth Corps**
Maj. Gen. Winfield S. Hancock	Maj. Gen. John Sedgewick
Uniontown, Maryland	Manchester, Maryland
Distance to Battlefield – 22 miles	Distance to Battlefield – 22 miles
Third Corps	**Eleventh Corps**
Maj. Gen. Daniel E. Sickles	Maj. Gen. Oliver O. Howard
Bridgeport, Maryland	Emmitsburg, Maryland
Distance to Battlefield – 12 miles	Distance to Battlefield – 11 miles

Twelfth Corps

Maj. Gen. Howard Slocum

Littlestown, Pennsylvania

Distance to Battlefield – 10 miles

Artillery Reserve

Brig. Gen. Robert Tyler

Taneytown, Maryland

Distance to Battlefield – 14 miles

Cavalry Corps Headquarters

Brig. Gen. Alfred Pleasonton

Taneytown, Maryland

Distance to Battlefield – 14 miles

First Cavalry Division

Brig. Gen. John Buford

1st and 2nd Brigades

Gettysburg, Pennsylvania

Reserve Brigade

Brig. Gen. Wesley Merritt

Mechanicstown

[present-day Thurmont], Maryland

Distance to Battlefield – 20 miles

Second Cavalry Division

Brig. Gen. David M. Gregg

Manchester, Maryland

Distance to Battlefield – 22 miles

Third Cavalry Division

Brig. Gen. H. Judson Kilpatrick

Hanover, Pennsylvania

Distance to Battlefield – 14 miles

CONFEDERATE FORCES

ARMY OF NORTHERN VIRGINIA HEADQUARTERS

Gen. Robert E. Lee

Greenwood, Pennsylvania

Distance to Battlefield – 13 miles

First Corps

Lt. Gen. James Longstreet

McLaws' and Hood's Divisions

Greenwood, Pennsylvania

Distance to Battlefield – 13 miles

Pickett's Division

Chambersburg, Pennsylvania

Distance to Battlefield – 22 miles

Second Corps
Lt. Gen. Richard S. Ewell

Early's and Rodes' Divisions
Heidlersburg, Pennsylvania
Distance to Battlefield – 10 miles

Johnson's Division
Green Village, Pennsylvania
Distance to Battlefield – 23 miles

Third Corps
Lt. Gen. Ambrose P. Hill

Anderson's Division
Fayetteville, Pennsylvania
Distance to Battlefield – 12 miles

Heth's Division
Seven Stars - Cashtown, Pennsylvania
Distance to Battlefield – 5 to 6 miles

Pender's Division
Cashtown, Pennsylvania
Distance to Battlefield – 6 miles

Cavalry Division Headquarters
Maj. Gen. J.E.B. Stuart
Jefferson, Pennsylvania
Distance to Battlefield – 27 miles

**Fitz Lee's, W.H.F. Lee's
and Hampton's Brigades**
Jefferson, Pennsylvania
Distance to Battlefield – 27 miles

Imboden's Brigade
Hancock, Maryland
Distance to Battlefield – 49 miles

Jenkins' Brigade
Mechanicsburg, Pennsylvania
Distance to Battlefield – 29 miles

Jones' and Robertson's Brigades
Gaps of Lower Blue Ridge Mountains
Distance to Battlefield – 80 miles

Weather Conditions During the Battle of Gettysburg

Those who wish to know the weather conditions before, during and after the Battle of Gettysburg are thankful for the efforts of Rev. Dr. Michael Jacobs (1808-1871) *(right)*. A resident of the town since 1829, Jacobs was Professor of Mathematics and Natural Sciences at Pennsylvania College (now Gettysburg College) in July 1863. Jacobs began taking daily readings of weather conditions in Gettysburg in 1839 and continued until nearly his death. Following are his meteorological observations of the days before, during, and after the battle.

"The entire period of the invasion is remarkable for being one of clouds, and, for that season of the year, of low temperature. From June 15th until July 22nd, 1863, there was not an entirely clear day. On the evening of June 25th at 8 p.m. a rain began. This rain continued at intervals until Saturday June 27th, at 7 a.m., the perception being in inches 1.280. At all the observations made on Saturday and Sunday, and until the nine o'clock observation of Monday night, the entire sky was covered with clouds. On the day before the battle [Tuesday, June 30], both at 7 a.m., and 2 p.m., the obscuration was again complete, with cumulo-stratus clouds moving from SSE. At 9 p.m., only four-tenths of the heavens were covered . . . the records of the wind are those of almost entire calm."

Jacobs made his temperature observations three times per day. On June 30, the day before the battle began, Jacobs recorded the temperature at 7 a.m. to be 68°, at 2 p.m. it was 79°, and at 9 p.m. the temperature was 71°. He noted that there was "complete cloud cover all day, partly cleared by 9 p.m. Wind was calm." For the three days of the battle, Jacobs recorded the following observations:

July 1st

The entire sky was covered with clouds all day, cumulo-stratus at 7 a.m. and 2 p.m., cirro-stratus at 9 p.m. A very gentle southern breeze (2 mph). Thermometer: 7 a.m. – 72°; 2 p.m. – 76°; 9 p.m. – 74°

July 2nd

At 8 a.m., sky still covered (cumulo-stratus). At 2 p.m., 3/10 clear. At 9 p.m. cirrus clouds. Wind same as preceding day. Thermometer: 7 a.m. – 74°; 2 p.m. – 81°; 9 p.m. – 76°

July 3rd

At 8 a.m., sky again completely covered with cumulo-stratus clouds, at 2 p.m., sky on 4/10 covered, but with cumulus or the thunderclouds of summer; at 9 p.m., 7/10 cumulus. Wind SSW, very gentle. Thunderstorm in neighborhood at 6 p.m. The thunder seemed tame, after the artillery firing of the afternoon. Thermometer: 7 a.m. – 73°; 2 p.m. – 87°; 9 p.m. – 76°

Jacobs watched much of the battle in and surrounding the town through an observation window in the top of the roof of his West Middle Street home. Jacobs and his son, Henry, watched Pickett's Charge through the window on the afternoon of July 3. On July 4, as Robert E. Lee's army prepared to retreat from the battlefield, and the two armies cautiously watched each other for movement as rain showers moved in, Jacobs recorded the following observations for the day:

July 4th

Rain showers at 6 a.m., from 2:15 until 4 p.m., and at 4 a.m. on July 5 totaling 1.39 inches. Thermometer: 7 a.m. – 69°; 2 p.m. – 72°; 9 p.m. – 70°

Jacobs then noted that slight showers fell on the Gettysburg area on the 5th, 6th, and 7th, and on July 8 a steady rain fell from 3 a.m. until 11:30 a.m., totaling 1.3 inches. Days of steady rain and sloppy conditions made Lee's retreat to a rising Potomac River miserable for his soldiers. Quite interestingly, according to Jacobs' observations, the highest temperature during the entire month of July 1863 was 87° degrees; it was on the afternoon of July 3, just at about the very time that Pickett's Charge was stepping off toward the Federal lines.

Medal of Honor Awardees

The highest honor that an American soldier can be awarded, the Medal of Honor is also one of the world's most respected military medals. First authorized by Congress on December 21, 1861, nearly 3,500 American soldiers have been awarded the medal – either post-humously or during their lifetime. The Medal of Honor recognizes those selfless individuals who exhibited valor above and beyond the call of duty.

The Medal of Honor has its roots in the early years of the country, when Gen. George Washington established the Badge of Military Merit on August 7, 1782 to recognize acts of military gallantry during the Revolutionary War. It consisted of a purple cloth heart, and only three soldiers were ever presented the award. It was reinstated in 1932, and now is known as the Purple Heart.

The Medal of Honor began as an award for acts of valor in the United States Navy during the Civil War when Lincoln established it in 1861, then in July 1862 it was created to reward gallantry in all branches of the army. The award was made permanent by Congress the following year. Although a very few issuances of the medal during the Civil War were for political or recruitment purposes, or for acts that today don't seem so courageous, awardees since that war are, without excep-tion, true American heroes. Recipients are held by the American public and citizens throughout the world in the greatest respect. No less than famous Civil War general and Indian fighter George Armstrong Custer once offered to give up his rank for a medal; he never got one, but his brother Thomas, who died with George at the 1876 battle at the Little Big Horn, was awarded two of them during the Civil War.

Only one woman has ever been awarded a Medal of Honor. Mary E. Walker, a Civil War surgeon for the Federal Army, was awarded the medal at the end of the war for her efforts. She served as first a nurse at the beginning of the war, then as the first U.S. Army female surgeon. In April 1864, she crossed behind Rebel lines and was arrested by Confederates as a spy. She was exchanged in August and returned to her duties. In 1917, Congress rescinded the medal after investigations into non-combat awards of the medal, but it was officially reinstated by President Jimmy Carter in 1977.

A total of 64 Federal soldiers were awarded the Medal of Honor (the most recent, posthumously to Lt. Alonzo H. Cushing in 2010) for their acts of bravery during the three-day battle of Gettysburg. Following is an alphabetical list of their names (with rank at the time of the event), their unit (or command), and the act that garnered the medal.

CPL. NATHANIEL M. ALLEN
(1st Massachusetts Infantry)
July 2 – returned under fire to save
the regimental colors

PVT. ELIJAH W. BACON
(14th Connecticut Infantry)
July 3 – Captured the flag of the
16th North Carolina Infantry

LT. GEORGE G. BENEDICT
(12th Vermont Infantry)
July 3 – Passed through heavy artillery
fire to deliver orders and reformed
his regiment's lines

CAPT. MORRIS BROWN, JR.
(126th New York Infantry)
July 3 – Captured a Confederate flag

SGT. HUGH CAREY
(82nd New York Infantry)
July 2 – Wounded twice while capturing
the flag of the 7th Virginia Infantry

PVT. CASPER R. CARLISLE
(Pennsylvania Independent Lt. Artillery)
July 2 – Saved one of his battery's
guns while under a heavy fire

COL. JOSHUA L. CHAMBERLAIN
(20th Maine Infantry)
July 2 – Held his flank position on
Little Round Top after repeated assaults

CPL. HARRISON CLARK
(125th New York Infantry)
July 2 – Seized regimental colors and
advanced after color bearer had been shot

PVT. JOHN E. CLOPP
(71st Pennsylvania Infantry)
July 3 – Wrestled away the flag of the
9th Virginia Infantry from its color bearer

SGT. JEFFERSON COATES
(7th Wisconsin Infantry)
July 1 – Displayed courage in battle,
both of his eyes were shot out

LT. ALONZO H. CUSHING
(4th U.S. Artillery, Battery A)
July 3 – Remained with his guns even
though desperately wounded, finally
killed standing by his battery

CPL. JOSEPH H. DeCASTRO
(19th Massachusetts Infantry)
July 3 – Captured the flag of the
19th Virginia Infantry

SGT. GEORGE H. DORE
(126th New York Infantry)
July 3 – Saved his regiment's flag under
fire when the color bearer was shot down

MUSICIAN RICHARD ENDERLIN
(73rd Ohio Infantry)
July 1-3 – Took up a rifle voluntarily
and served in the ranks; went into
the enemy's lines at night and
rescued a wounded comrade

COLOR SGT. BENJAMIN F. FALLS
(19th Massachusetts Infantry)
July 3 – Captured a Confederate flag

CAPT. JOHN B. FASSETT
(23rd Pennsylvania Infantry)
July 2 – Voluntarily led another
regiment to assist an artillery battery,
recaptured the guns from the enemy

CPL. CHRISTOPHER FLYNN
(14th Connecticut Infantry)
July 3 – Captured the flag of the
52nd North Carolina Infantry

SGT. FREDERICK FUGER
(Sergeant, 4th U.S. Artillery Battery A)
July 3 – After all officers of his battery
were killed or wounded and five of
the guns disabled, he fought with the
remaining gun until it was ordered
withdrawn

CPL. CHESTER S. FURMAN
(6th Pennsylvania Reserves)
July 2 – With five other volunteers,
charged and captured a squad of
Confederate sharpshooters

SGT. EDWARD L. GILLIGAN
(88th Pennsylvania Infantry)
July 1 – Knocked down a
Confederate color bearer and
helped to capture his flag

SGT. JOHN W. HART
(6th Pennsylvania Reserves)
July 2 – With five other volunteers,
charged and captured a squad of
Confederate sharpshooters

SGT. MAJ. WILLIAM B. HINCKS
(14th Connecticut Infantry)
July 3 – Captured the flag of the
14th Tennessee Infantry

SGT. THOMAS HORAN
(72nd New York Infantry)
July 2 – Captured the flag of the
8th Florida Infantry

LT. COL. HENRY S. HUIDEKOPER
(150th Pennsylvania Infantry)
July 1 – Remained in command of his
regiment even while severely wounded

CAPT. FRANCIS IRSCH
(45th New York Infantry)
July 1 – Led his men in flanking the
enemy and holding part of the town while
the army rallied atop Cemetery Hill

SGT. BENJAMIN H. JELLISON
(19th Massachusetts Infantry)
July 3 – Captured the flag of the
57th Virginia Infantry

9

SGT. WALLACE W. JOHNSON
(6th Pennsylvania Reserves)
July 2 – With five other volunteers, charged and captured a squad of Confederate sharpshooters

LT. EDWARD M. KNOX
(15th New York Artillery Battery)
July 2 – Severely wounded while staying with his guns after all other batteries had retired

CAPT. JOHN LONERGAN
(13th Vermont Infantry)
July 2 – Led in the recapture of four artillery pieces, and two of the enemy's guns

PVT. JOHN B. MAYBERRY
(1st Delaware Infantry)
July 3 – Captured a Confederate flag

PVT. BERNARD McCARREN
(1st Delaware Infantry)
July 3 – Captured a Confederate flag

SGT. GEORGE W. MEARS
(6th Pennsylvania Reserves)
July 2 – With five other volunteers, charged and captured a squad of Confederate sharpshooters

CPT. JOHN MILLER
(8th Ohio Infantry)
July 3 – Captured two Confederate flags

CAPT. WILLIAM E. MILLER
(3rd Pennsylvania Cavalry)
July 3 – Led his squadron in an attack without orders, and cut off the rear of the Confederate cavalry column

SGT. HARVEY M. MUNSELL
(99th Pennsylvania Infantry)
July 1-3 – Courage displayed as color bearer (carried the flag through 13 battles)

CPL. HENRY D. O'BRIEN
(1st Minnesota Infantry)
July 3 – Took up his regiment's flag after the color bearer was shot, charged the enemy and was wounded twice

SGT. JAMES PIPES
(140th Pennsylvania Infantry)
July 2 – Severely wounded while carrying a wounded comrade

SGT. GEORGE C. PLATT
(6th U.S. Cavalry)
July 3 – Saved the regimental flag in a hand-to-hand fight

CAPT. JAMES P. POSTLES
(1st Delaware Infantry)
July 2 – Voluntarily delivered an order under heavy fire

LT. JAMES J. PURMAN
(140th Pennsylvania Infantry)
July 2 – Severely wounded while carrying a wounded comrade

CPL. WILLIAM H. RAYMOND
(108th New York Infantry)
July 3 – Voluntarily delivered a box of ammunition under heavy fire to the skirmish line

BUGLER CHARLES W. REED
(9th Independent Battery, Massachusetts Light Artillery)
July 2 – Rescued his wounded captain from between the lines

CPL. J. MONROE REISINGER
(150th Pennsylvania Infantry)
July 1 – Specially brave and
meritorious conduct

MAJ. EDMUND RICE
(19th Massachusetts Infantry)
July 3 – Countercharged the
Confederates and was severely wounded

PVT. JAMES RICHMOND
(8th Ohio Infantry)
July 3 – Captured a Confederate flag

PVT. JOHN H. ROBINSON
(19th Massachusetts Infantry)
July 3 – Captured the flag of the
57th Virginia Infantry

PVT. OLIVER P. ROOD
(20th Indiana Infantry)
July 3 – Captured the flag of the
21st North Carolina Infantry

SGT. GEORGE W. ROOSEVELT
(26th Pennsylvania Infantry)
July 2 – Captured a Confederate
color bearer and flag, and was
severely wounded

CPL. J. LEVI ROUSH
(6th Pennsylvania Reserves)
July 2 – With five other volunteers,
charged and captured a squad of
Confederate sharpshooters

SGT. JAMES M. RUTTER
(143rd Pennsylvania Infantry)
July 1 – Carried a wounded comrade
to safety under fire

PVT. MARTIN SCHWENK
[REAL NAME GEORGE MARTIN]
(6th U.S. Cavalry)
July 3 – Rescued a wounded officer
from the enemy

MAJ. ALFRED J. SELLERS
(90th Pennsylvania Infantry)
July 1 – Led his regiment in a
countercharge under a heavy fire

PVT. MARSHALL SHERMAN
(1st Minnesota Infantry)
July 3 – Captured the flag of the
28th Virginia Infantry

MAJ. GEN. DANIEL E. SICKLES
(III Corps)
July 2 – Gallantry while contesting
Confederate assault, and encouraging his
corps after being severely wounded

CPL. THADDEUS S. SMITH
(6th Pennsylvania Reserves)
July 2 – With five other volunteers,
charged and captured a squad of
Confederate sharpshooters

PVT. CHARLES STACEY
(55th Ohio Infantry)
July 2 – Voluntarily advanced to
the skirmish line under fire to reconnoiter
the Confederate position

SGT. JAMES B. THOMPSON
(1st Pennsylvania Rifles)
July 3 – Captured the flag of the
15th Georgia Infantry

SGT. ANDREW J. TOZIER
(20th Maine Infantry)
July 2 – While holding the flag as
color bearer, picked up rifles and
ammunition and fired at Confederates
as they charged his position

COL. WHEELOCK G. VEAZEY
(16th Vermont Infantry)
July 3 – Led his regiment in a flanking
charge, then a frontal assault, and
destroyed a Confederate brigade

PVT. JERRY WALL
(126th New York Infantry)
July 3 – Captured a Confederate flag

CPL. FRANCIS A. WALLER
(6th Wisconsin Infantry)
July 1 – Captured the flag of the
2nd Mississippi Infantry

BRIG. GEN. ALEXANDER S. WEBB
(2nd Brigade of 2nd Division, II Corps)
July 3 – Gallantly led his men forward
into hand-to-hand combat

MAJ. WILLIAM WELLS
(1st Vermont Cavalry)
July 3 – Personally led his battalion on a
mounted charge into Confederate lines

SGT. JAMES WILEY
(59th New York Infantry)
July 3 – Captured a Confederate flag
of a Georgia regiment

Gettysburg Trivia

Large numbers of Confederates arrived at Gettysburg from the **north**, while most of the Federals marched to the field from the **south**.

By July 3, the last day of the battle, there were some 150,000 military animals (horses and mules) on the battlefield. Put another way, there was almost as many animals as there were men.

(DEB MCCAUSLIN)

The first Federal soldier killed close to Gettysburg was **Pvt. George W. Sandoe** *(left)*, a member of a local militia cavalry unit raised of Adams County men. On July 26, 1863, Sandoe and several dozen of Capt. Robert Bell's Adams County Cavalry were chased through town by Confederate cavalrymen on their way toward the Susquehanna River. Sandoe was shot dead along the Baltimore Pike about one mile southeast of town.

Approximately 3,500 horses and mules were killed during the three days of fighting. Many remained on the field for days and even weeks after the battle. Most of the rotting carcasses were burned and what was left was buried.

The first Confederate killed close to Gettysburg was shot by civilians near the Cashtown Pass a few miles west of town. **Pvt. Eli Amick** of the 14th Virginia Cavalry was on a foraging expedition with his fellow troopers on June 23, 1863 when four men ambushed the cavalrymen. He was shot in the stomach and died later that day.

Command of the Federal forces on the battlefield changed seven times during the first day of fighting on July 1. First in command was **Brig. Gen. John Buford**, who led the cavalry that opened the fighting. When **Maj. Gen. John F. Reynolds** reached the field with elements of his I Corps of infantry later that morning, he assumed command until he was killed a short time later. Command then devolved to one of Reynolds' division commanders, **Maj. Gen. Abner Doubleday**. The next change occurred when **Maj. Gen. Oliver O. Howard** of the XI Corps arrived on the field. Although junior in rank to Howard, **Maj. Gen. Winfield S. Hancock** (commanding the II Corps) assumed command after he arrived when ordered to do so by army commander **Maj. Gen. George G. Meade**. Early that evening, Hancock left the field to return to Taneytown, Maryland, to report the battlefield conditions to Meade, and thereby relinquished command. **Maj. Gen. Henry W. Slocum**, the head of the XII Corps, outranked Howard and took command when he arrived on the field that evening. Meade arrived on the battlefield sometime shortly after midnight to assume final command.

On July 2, **Col. John R. Towers** (whose regimental nickname was "Grandma") led his 8th Georgia Infantry during its attack on Federals in the

Wheatfield on George Rose's farm. More than fifty percent of his men became casualties, including Towers (who was slightly wounded). July 2 was the colonel's 39th birthday.

———————————

Sgt. Russel C. Mitchell of the 1st Texas Infantry participated in the assault against Devils' Den and Little Round Top on July 2. Russel was the grandfather of **Margaret Mitchell**, the author of *Gone With The Wind*.

———————————

Lt. Col. Jonathan H. Lockwood commanded the 7th West Virginia Infantry of the Federal army at Gettysburg. On July 3, his regiment helped defend the Union center during Pickett's Charge. The 7th captured a number of Confederates from Virginia regiments. It is reported that one of the captives was Lockwood's own nephew.

———————————

It is well known that **George E. Pickett**, the general for whom the grand July 3 Confederate infantry charge at Gettysburg is named, graduated last in his West Point Class (of 59 cadets) of 1846. Less well known is that his corps commander, **Lt. Gen. James Longstreet**, graduated 54th of 56 cadets in his West Point Class of 1842 – third from the bottom.

———————————

Estimates vary, but both sides together expended about 566 tons of ammunition (both small arms and artillery) during the three days of fighting. Put another way, twenty-four pounds of metal was launched into the air, one way or another, for each man who fell killed or wounded there.

———————————

Tons of armaments and equipment littered the battlefield after the fighting ended. Nearly 38,000 discarded rifles were collected and sent to Washington, D.C. to be inspected and fixed, if possible. Of that number, some 24,000 were found to be still loaded: 6,000 had one round in the barrel; 12,000 had two rounds in the barrel; the remaining 6,000 rifles had three to as many as ten rounds stuffed into the barrel, one on top of another. During the excitement of battle, soldiers sometimes loaded a round, forgot to fire, and then loaded their rifle again. Occasionally, they even neglected to remove their ramrod, which would be lost when the gun was finally fired. The most remarkable rifle of all had twenty-three rounds loaded into it, which filled the barrel all the way to the muzzle.

The tallest general in the Federal army at Gettysburg was **Brig. Gen. John W. Geary**, who commanded a division in the XII Corps. His 6'6" frame towered over nearly every man he ever met, including **President Abraham Lincoln**, who was two inches shorter.

Only one civilian was killed during the entire battle of Gettysburg when an errant bullet strick **Mary Virginia Wade** while she was in a home baking bread. Although she is famous today as "Jennie," her family and friends called her "Ginnie," the proper nickname for "Virginia."

The first marker or "monument" placed on the battlefield may be a handmade inscription carved into a boulder on the summit of Little Round Top. Just north of the large castle-like monument of the 12th and 44th New York Infantry is a large boulder on which is carved "Col. Strong Vincent fell here . . . July 2, 1863." **Colonel Vincent** was mortally wounded while standing on a boulder encouraging his men during the Confederate assault. The first public notice of the inscription's existence was in October 1864 when journalists from Vincent's hometown of Erie, Pennsylvania, spotted it during a visit to the battlefield.

The first regimental monument anywhere on the battlefield, and the first official memorial of any kind, was placed in 1867. It is a stone urn at the head of the state of Minnesota graves section in the Soldiers' National Cemetery, dedicated to the **1st Minnesota Infantry**.

A short distance south of the "High Water Mark" and Copse of Trees along Cemetery Ridge is a monument featuring a brass plaque with a relief of the July 3 Pickett's Charge attack. In the right corner of the plaque is a Confederate flag, the first of its kind to appear on the battlefield. Ironically, the flag is on the **1st New York Independent Battery** monument, dedicated in 1887.

The **20th Massachusetts Infantry** monument along Cemetery Ridge is made of a large boulder that formerly stood in a Roxbury, Massachusetts, playground where many of the regiment's members played as children. The daughter of the 20th's commander donated the bronze tablet on the base of the monument as a gift. The commander's name was **Col. Paul J. Revere**, who was mortally wounded on July 2. He was the grandson of the famous Revolutionary War patriot.

At age 62, **Brig. Gen. George S. Greene** was the oldest Federal general at Gettysburg. His brigade fought valiantly on Culp's Hill on July 2 and 3. He died in 1899 at the age of 97, and his headstone atop his grave in Kent County, Rhode Island, is a boulder from Culp's Hill.

In order to faithfully create the statue of **Gen. Robert E. Lee's** horse **Traveller** atop the Virginia Memorial (dedicated in 1917), sculptor **Frederick Sievers** visited Traveller's skeleton on display at Washington and

Lee University in Virginia. He used the skeleton to find a horse matching Traveller's size and shape, and then used it to model his famous statue.

⁂

Contrary to popular myth, **President Abraham Lincoln** did not write his speech while on the train from Washington, D.C. to Gettysburg, nor did he write it on the back of an envelope. He wrote most of the speech in Washington on Executive Mansion stationery during the two weeks prior to the ceremony. The president likely put some finishing touches on it while staying at the Gettysburg home of attorney **David Wills** the night before the dedication.

⁂

At the November 19, 1863, dedication of the **Soldiers' National Cemetery** at Gettysburg, **President Lincoln** did not actually deliver his famous address in the cemetery itself. Modern photographic analysis reveals that the speaker's platform was erected in the adjacent town burial ground called **Evergreen Cemetery**. The platform was erected to look out toward the new cemetery, in which fresh graves were still being dug during the ceremony.

⁂

Lincoln had been suffering for days from a mild form of smallpox, known as *variola minor*, when he arrived in Gettysburg to deliver his famous address. On the train to Gettysburg on November 18, 1863, Lincoln complained to his private secretary, **John Hay**, that he felt weak and sore. After the Gettysburg event Lincoln suffered from further symptoms common to the disease, including high fever, headache, and skin blisters. It was a serious disease that claimed the lives of some one-third of its victims. Lincoln of course survived, only to be assassinated by **John Wilkes Booth** in April 1865.

⁂

No Confederate dead were to have been buried in the **Soldiers' National Cemetery**, but as many as nine Southerners are mistakenly interred there. Initial burials on the field were often hastily performed, unmarked, misidentified, or marked with inscriptions difficult to read. This led to errors in the recording of names and units. Most of these Confederates have been identified today.

Today, the **Gettysburg National Military Park** encompasses nearly 6,000 acres of land, although many actions and troop movements directly related to the fighting ranged over a much wider area of Adams County.

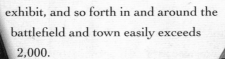

The Gettysburg Battlefield is the most commemorated field in the United States, and perhaps the entire world. The grand total for every monument, memorial, marker, historical signage, wayside exhibit, and so forth in and around the battlefield and town easily exceeds 2,000.

Controversies, Myths, and Misconceptions about the Gettysburg Campaign and Battle

Gettysburg, perhaps more than any other battle of the war, has given rise to a legion of controversies, misconceptions, and myths. Most are the result of faulty memories, spanning the spectrum from the innocently inaccurate to bald-face lies. In some cases these inaccuracies have been romanticized and embellished or simply perpetuated by writers and historians during and after the war. Many are now cemented into the public consciousness, true or otherwise. Some controversies rage even today and are unlikely to be resolved any time soon. Following are a few of the most interesting, the most common, or at least the most . . . persistent.

Did the battle begin on July 1 by "accident" because Confederate Maj. Gen. Henry Heth, whose division of infantry opened the fighting west of town that morning, was marching toward Gettysburg looking for shoes?

THE BATTLE WAS NOT AN ACCIDENT and Heth was not looking for shoes. By the night of June 30 (the night before the start of the battle), Federal cavalry commander John Buford was in Gettysburg and knew the general whereabouts of most of the larger pieces of the Confederate army. About midday on June 30, as Buford's cavalry column was riding into town, a lone Confederate infantry brigade was spotted west of Gettysburg. Federal troopers followed as the Southerners withdrew along the Chambersburg Pike toward Cashtown. Interviews with local citizens and intelligence gathered by troopers reconnoitering several miles to the west and north convinced Buford that the bulk of Robert E. Lee's Army of Northern Virginia was not too far distant in those directions. Buford predicted that Confederates would move on Gettysburg the following morning (July 1) from the west, and that more Rebels would likely arrive from the west. Gettysburg was an important hub for many important roads, and holding it offered either army the ability to move quickly in any direction. Buford was right. That is exactly what happened the next day.

As for the Confederates, General Lee had recently received information that the Federal Army of the Potomac had crossed north of the Potomac River and was thus much closer to his own separated army than he previously believed. Neither Lee nor Federal commander George G. Meade expected a major battle to erupt at Gettysburg on July 1, but it is not true the two armies simply blundered into each other by accident.

Regarding the oft-told tale of Confederates looking for shoes at Gettysburg, it is true the Southerners were in sore need of footwear and many other sundry items. However, there was no large collection of shoes stockpiled at Gettysburg, and no one expected to discover any in quantity there. After the battle, Heth wrote that he marched his men to Gettysburg on the morning of July 1 to find supplies and "shoes, especially," just as many elements of the Southern army had been doing while operating in Maryland and Pennsylvania. Over the years, Heth's statement has been romanticized (and compressed) into the tale that Confederates marched on the town only to find shoes. Heth and his corps commander, Lt. Gen. Ambrose P. Hill, also had information that a Federal presence had been spotted in town. Historians have speculated that Hill and Heth deduced that the enemy troops were only local militia that could be brushed easily aside, and the town could then be ransomed for useful supplies.

Who fired the first shot to start the Gettysburg battle?

THE FIRST SHOT FIRED WAS FIRED by a Federal in the direction of massed Confederate troops moving east toward Gettysburg. That shot was almost certainly fired by Lt. Marcellus Jones of the 8th Illinois Cavalry. Over the years, many others claimed to have fired the "first shot" to open the battle.

After the war, and especially during the active period of monument placement at Gettysburg in the 1890s, several soldiers from various regiments of Federal Brig. Gen. John Buford's cavalry division argued about who fired that "first shot." Cpl. Alpheus Hodges of the 9th New York Cavalry claimed he fired the opening shot at Confederate skirmishers he confronted early on the morning of July 1. He stated that he and other troopers from his regiment were posted along the Chambersburg Pike when they spotted Confederate infantry approaching. They fired at Hodges, and Hodges returned fire before retiring to alert the rest of Buford's cavalry. However, neither Hodges nor any of the troopers of the 9th New York Cavalry were posted along the Chambersburg Pike that morning. Vedettes (forward outposts) from that regiment were posted along the Newville Road to the north. If Hodges spotted and fired at Southerners, they may have been stragglers from Lt. Gen. Richard Ewell's Confederate corps, a division of which had passed through the Gettysburg area a few days earlier. Several members of the 17th Pennsylvania Cavalry of Buford's division also made similar "first shot" claims, but any Confederates they may have confronted early that morning were not members of a massed Southern infantry advance.

Lt. Marcellus Jones, however, was in command of the 8th Illinois Cavalry forward outposts along the Chambersburg Pike on the morning of July 1. Maj. Gen. Henry Heth's Confederate division approached along that road from Cashtown to Gettysburg, and confronted Lt. Jones' outpost atop Knoxlyn Ridge four miles west of town. To mark the spot of his first shot, in 1886 Jones and a few of his comrades placed a small granite marker in the side yard of the home of Ephraim Wisler along the Cashtown Pike during the battle. The marker can be seen today on the north side of the intersection of the pike (modern Rt. 30) and Knoxlyn Road, and is known to many Gettysburg students and historians as the "First Shot Marker."

Given all the evidence, Lt. Jones holds the honor of firing a few ounces of lead that opened a battle that would witness the unleashing of tons of ammunition in and around Gettysburg over the next three days.

Was Brig. Gen. John Buford's Federal cavalry armed with repeating carbines on July 1, thus giving them an advantage that enabled them to delay a vastly superior force of Confederate infantry during the opening stages of the battle?

ONE OF THE MORE ENDURING MYTHS about Buford's cavalry at Gettysburg is that his troopers were armed with the fast-firing breech-loading Spencer carbine. The Spencer carbine, a lever-action repeating weapon loaded with self-contained cartridges, did not go into mass production until after the Gettysburg Campaign ended. Buford's cavalry was armed with a variety of single-shot breech-loading carbines, each of which had to be manually fed a paper- or linen-wrapped cartridge. A company or more of the 17th Pennsylvania Cavalry in Buford's division may have been armed with the longer Spencer rifle (which had been in production for two years), but no Spencer shell casings have ever been discovered on that part of the field. Although they were vastly outnumbered until Federal infantry from the I Corps arrived, Buford's troopers were able to delay the Confederate advance by deploying on well-selected ridges and maintaining an incessant level of fire, thereby forcing the Confederates to deploy to engage them. After holding as long as possible, the troopers would then retire to the next suitable rise to the east and repeat the process.

One cavalry regiment (and part of another) in Brig. Gen. George A. Custer's brigade were armed with the repeating Spencer rifle, but that brigade was not present on July 1. It fought a battle at Hunterstown, Pennsylvania, on July 2 and on East Cavalry Field on July 3.

It is often said that the Confederates had no cavalry with them on the first day of the battle. Was any Confederate cavalry present with the Southern infantry on the battlefield on July 1 and if so, how was it used?

YES. TWO SMALL BUT ABLE AND experienced forces of Confederate cavalry were with Lt. Gen. Richard S. Ewell's Corps when it arrived on the battlefield on the afternoon of July 1.

Much of the criticism leveled against Confederate cavalry commander Maj. Gen. J.E.B. Stuart is that he took "all" of the Southern cavalry with him on his pre-Gettysburg ride through Virginia, Maryland, and Pennsylvania, during which he lost contact with the main Confederate army. In fact, Stuart took just over one-half (three brigades) of the available cavalry force plus just six horse artillery guns with him. Two cavalry organizations that remained with the Confederate infantry—the 17th Virginia Cavalry and the 35th Battalion Virginia Cavalry—accompanied Lt. Gen. Richard S. Ewell's Corps' during its march into Pennsylvania. Col. William French's 17th Virginia troopers were veteran fighters skilled at reconnaissance, and there were few better at scouting than the 250 members of Lt. Col. Elijah V. White's 35th Battalion. Both units, totaling about 500 cavalry, came onto the battlefield on the afternoon of July 1 with Ewell's infantry and could have been used to scout Federal positions and movements. They could also have made a detailed reconnaissance of the developing Federal defensive positions at Culp's Hill and Cemetery Hill. The historian of White's Battalion later lamented that the cavalrymen were instead used only to round up prisoners and otherwise only to observe the fighting.

Was Federal Maj. Gen. John F. Reynolds, the highest ranking Federal officer killed during the battle, shot by a Rebel sharpshooter?

WE WILL NEVER KNOW WITH COMPLETE certainty, but it is unlikely. After the battle, stories of the gallant Reynolds being felled by a skilled Rebel sharpshooter became commonplace. One even claimed that a Confederate crack shot, perched in a tree 800 yards away, drew his sights on the officer and brought him down. Several Southerners after the war claimed to have been the sharpshooter. At the time Reynolds was shot, however, he was mounted and leading troops into a stand of woods east of the Edward McPherson farm. Heavy tree cover would have prevented any Confederate from seeing him from such a distance. Right before Reynolds was hit, a general volley of musket fire exploded from the front ranks of Confederate infantry under Brig. Gen. James Archer. Many soldiers around Reynolds were also killed or wounded at the same general time. It is much more likely that the commander of the I Corps was shot and killed by a bullet fired during that volley rather than by a sharpshooter specifically aiming for that officer.

Did a shot from Capt. Hubert Dilger's Federal artillery battery fired on July 1 hit and lodge in the muzzle of a Confederate cannon posted atop Oak Hill?

THIS IS ONE OF THE OFTEN repeated and very dramatic stories of the first day of battle. While supporting Federal infantry posted north of Gettysburg on the afternoon of July 1, Capt. Dilger fired a cannon shot at Southern artillery posted on Oak Hill. When that first shot flew high and the Rebels shouted and waved derisively at Dilger, the story goes, the captain lined up another shot, which dismounted one of the Confederate guns. The Federal officer then aimed and fired a third shot. A Federal infantry colonel asked him, "What effect, Captain Dilger?" After looking through his field glass for some time, Dilger is said to have replied, "I have spiked a gun for them, plugging it at the muzzle." In other words, the round flew directly into the muzzle of one of Captain Richard Page's guns and knocked it out of service.

The legend originally circulated when the story of a Federal soldier, claiming to have seen the "spiked" cannon, appeared in a book of North Carolina's service during the war. Supposedly the Federal, who was taken prisoner on July 1, spotted the damaged gun and saw that the muzzle was "split." The story then was embellished with the conversation between Dilger and the unidentified infantry officer. Dilger, however, never made such a claim in his report or in any other writings. Neither did anyone else on either side, including those responsible for Southern ordnance reports. Finally, it would have been all but impossible for Dilger to see the effect of such a miraculous shot from his position because he was several hundred yards away using only four-power binoculars while looking through very heavy powder smoke.

Did Capt. Samuel Johnston, who was sent by Gen. Robert E. Lee on a ride during the pre-dawn hours of July 2 to discover the location of the Federal left flank, make it all the way to Little Round Top and back to Confederate lines undetected?

DEBATE ON THIS ISSUE CONTINUES TO this day, but it seems fairly certain that Johnston did not reach Little Round Top. About 4:00 a.m. on July 2, Johnston left with a small party, crossed the Emmitsburg Road, and continued toward the Round Tops in an effort to determine the disposition of the Federal army in that sector. When he returned, Johnston reported that he had ridden up a hill later known as Little Round Top, and that there were no Federal troops in that sector. Was that possible?

We know that a Federal signal station was located on Little Round Top by that time, and that Federal troops had been marching up the Emmitsburg Road during the night to their positions. In addition, cavalry outposts from John Buford's command were posted all along Cemetery Ridge between the Confederate and Federal positions. These facts make it difficult to determine how it was that Johnston and his party could have made their way undetected through so many Federal obstacles and onto a hill manned by at least signal personnel. If Johnston rode a considerable distance east of the Emmitsburg Road and thus toward the developing Federal line, he may have ended his foray much farther south than Little Round Top. There is no evidence that Johnston offered an intentionally false story to deceive his superiors. What is certain is that he was not familiar with the terrain, and owing to the darkness may have assumed that he made it onto or very close to the hill in question. Some historians offer the theory that if he successfully navigated a route that far east of the Emmitsburg Road, Johnston may have reached Big Round Top or perhaps Bushman's Hill, both south of Little Round Top.

By the time the late afternoon Confederate assault against the Federal left flank got underway on July 2, the situation there had fundamentally changed. By that time Federal Maj. Gen. Daniel E. Sickles had advanced most of his III Corps toward the Emmitsburg Road, far ahead of the rest of the Federal line immediately to his north on Cemetery Ridge. The presence of an entire enemy corps that far forward surprised the attacking Confederates.

<hr />

Did Confederate Lt. Gen. James Longstreet receive a "dawn order" from Gen. Robert E. Lee to attack on July 2?

THERE IS NO RELIABLE OR CONVINCING evidence that Longstreet received an order to prepare for an attack that day before about 11:00 a.m., and especially not during the early dawn. A target on several fronts during the "Lost Cause" era following the war, Longstreet was criticized by several former Confederate officers for not launching his attack (which began about 4:00 p.m.) earlier on July 2. Historians have deeply examined the actions and movements of Lee, his staff, Longstreet, and his subordinate officers present on the field at the time. After spending several hours from early dawn reconnoitering and discussing the terrain on the Confederate right (the southern part of the battlefield) with his subordinates, Lee issued his official order for Longstreet to prepare for an attack about 11:00 a.m.

It took time for Longstreet to get his troops to their assigned positions on the southern part of the field. Some of his troops made what historians have nicknamed "Longstreet's Countermarch"—an unplanned semi-circular countermarch in the area of the Black Horse Tavern, because his troops were initially spotted by the Federal signal station on Little Round Top. After countermarching and taking an alternate and less visible route, Longstreet's troops reached their jump-off positions by the middle of the afternoon. Once Longstreet launched his assault about 4:00 p.m., he attacked with a vigor that validated Lee's sobriquet for his trusted lieutenant: "My Old War Horse." The complexity of the large-scale assault and success it garnered that day, however, did not deter proponents of the "Lost Cause" from accusing Longstreet of intentionally dragging his feet on July 2. By doing so, they hoped to heap much of the blame for the loss at Gettysburg, and by extension the entire war, onto his shoulders and thus off the back of General Lee.

***

When Maj. Gen. Daniel E. Sickles marched most of his Federal III Corps from its position at the southern end of the Federal line forward to the Emmitsburg Road on July 2, did he disobey orders and was the move tactically sound?

"SICKLES' ADVANCE" IS PERHAPS THE BEST known controversy of the battle. Literally hundreds of books, articles, and web pages have addressed the issue. Even though it has been examined from what appears to be every conceivable angle, Gettysburg enthusiasts remain divided on this issue.

On July 2, the position Sickles' 10,000-man corps was supposed to occupy was on the left flank of the Federal line along lower Cemetery Ridge. His left flank was supposed to rest at Little Round Top, and his right flank was to connect with Maj. Gen. Winfield S. Hancock's II Corps farther north on Cemetery Ridge. Sickles, however, did not like his assigned position because much of his front was lower than the ground west of his position, including Houck's Ridge and a slight ridge that ran along the Emmitsburg Road. Sickles was also worried that his own left flank could be attacked and turned by Confederates.

After attempting to get Maj. Gen. George G. Meade, the Army of the Potomac's commander, to pay attention to his concerns, Sickles—on his own volition—moved most of his corps a half mile forward (directly west) to the Emmitsburg Road. This position was roughly the midway point between the opposing armies' main lines. Many Federals, including Maj. Gen. Hancock, were surprised when they saw Sickles' troops marching so far forward of the main battle line. By the time his line was formed, Sickles' III Corps drew an extended front with part of his command facing generally west along the road, and the balance facing generally southwest from the Peach Orchard through Devil's Den, with the orchard itself forming a weak and vulnerable salient.

When Meade learned of the move he told Sickles that his troops were too far advanced and they discussed returning to the former line. Within minutes, however, Confederate artillery opened fire on the advanced position in preparation for Lt. Gen. James Longstreet's infantry assault that would follow. Unable to withdraw, Sickles' men were attacked and overwhelmed. Significant reinforcements from other parts of the Union line were needed to stabilize the left flank and keep that portion of the battlefield from falling into Southern hands. By the time the fighting ended some 40% of Sickles' corps had been killed, wounded, or captured. Sickles suffered a crippling leg wound from an artillery round and the limb was later amputated.

Historians argue about whether Sickles disobeyed orders by moving forward on his own. According to Meade, the advanced position was not the line he "intended" and "expected" Sickles to occupy. There is also the question of whether Sickles' advanced position absorbed Longstreet's assault farther from Cemetery Ridge, and in doing so, dissipated much of its power that might otherwise have rolled over the ridge farther north and Little Round Top. Although this question can never be definitively answered, what is indisputable is that any advantage gained by Sickles' advance was paid in the coin of heavy casualties. Sickles' III Corps suffered, by far, more casualties that day than any other Union corps.

Daniel Sickles himself colors the debates surrounding his battle actions. The larger-than-life politician-turned-soldier was the only corps commander in the Army of the Potomac who was not a West Pointer. His personal life before, during, and after the war was filled with one scandal after another. He is even suspected of having embezzled the funds provided to erect a bust of him on a battlefield monument. Sickles redeemed some of his shady reputation, however, by playing an instrumental role in preserving much of the battlefield so that it can be studied and enjoyed today. He remains one of the most colorful – and hotly debated – figures of Gettysburg lore.

Did Federal Col. Joshua L. Chamberlin and the 20th Maine Infantry "save the Federal Army" with their defense of Little Round Top on July 2?

JOSHUA CHAMBERLAIN AND HIS BRAVE LITTLE regiment fought admirably to help save Little Round Top, the important hill anchoring the left flank of the Federal army. The colonel and his men were placed on the end of the Federal left flank just as infantry from Lt. Gen. James Longstreet's Confederate corps began attacking the southern spur of Little Round Top. After valiantly repulsing several attacks on that part of the hill, the Maine troops ran low on ammunition. Chamberlain ordered his regiment to fix bayonets and some of his men began descending the hill to retrieve their wounded. Apparently without orders to do so (the record is unclear on this point), the men of the 20th Maine charged down the slope and into the attacking Confederate troops who, according to their commander Col. William Oates, were already beginning to retreat from the area. It was a stunning, if small scale, tactical victory and Chamberlain had handled his regiment with tremendous ability. There were no further attacks against that part of the hill.

Several books have featured the actions of the 20th Maine on July 2, notably Michael Shaara's Pulitzer Prize-winning *Killer Angels* (upon which the 1993 movie *Gettysburg* was based). As a result, what had been a little-known deed of bravery by a Maine regiment led by an obscure commander was catapulted into the national consciousness. If the Confederates had captured or gained a foothold on Little Round Top, the odds are they would not have held it for long. It may have posed some danger to the rest of the Federal line, but as an artillery platform or staging area it was not worth much to the attacking Southern army. In fact, Little Round Top was much more useful to the army holding the ground from that point northward. Farther north along the hill, several other Federal regiments were fighting to defend the western slope of Little Round Top, but their deeds are often overshadowed by the attention given to Chamberlain and his courageous men. *Killer Angels* and other books, films, and media have elevated the importance of this small-unit action beyond the reality of the situation. Chamberlain's actions were heroic, but he did not "save the Federal army" from defeat that afternoon.

Did Federal and Confederate soldiers drink from Spangler's Spring at the same time?

ONE OF THE MANY ROMANTICIZED TALES that grew out of Gettysburg battle lore is that during the night of July 2-3, soldiers of both sides motivated by a spirit of brotherhood despite the bloodshed that had taken place, congregated peacefully around the cool spring waters and drank together.

The area surrounding Spangler's Spring at the southern base of Culp's Hill changed hands several times during the battle. It was often situated in the dangerous "no man's land" between the two lines. The side that controlled the area enjoyed the use of the water. It is possible that in order to quench a powerful thirst, opposing soldiers may have visited the spring at the same time during the hours of darkness. But stories of the blue and gray joining together at the spring for some noble fraternal respite during the battle are untrue, yet understandable, byproducts of the efforts at reconciliation that followed the war.

Was the fighting at East Cavalry Field on July 3 mainly a battle of Brig. Gen. George A. Custer and his troopers against the Confederate cavalry?

CUSTER USUALLY GETS MOST OF THE credit due to his name recognition today, but the Federal cavalry commander on that field was Brig. Gen. David M. Gregg, commander of the Second Cavalry Division. Custer's brigade belonged to Brig. Gen. H. Judson Kilpatrick's Third Cavalry Division. When Kilpatrick's division came onto the battlefield from the east at midday on July 3, his other brigade (commanded by Brig. Gen. Elon J. Farnsworth) rode to the left flank of the Federal army. When Custer's brigade came up a short time later, Gregg suspected that he was going to be attacked by Confederate cavalry on the right flank, and in fact had seen dismounted Rebel cavalrymen beginning to form against him. Even though he outranked Custer, Gregg only asked Custer to remain with him on the right near the road to Hanover. Custer agreed.

Not long thereafter, Gregg was attacked in force by most of Maj. Gen. J.E.B. Stuart's Confederate cavalry (led by Stuart himself) on that flank near the John Rummel farm. Custer played a large role with Gregg's own two brigades in repulsing Stuart's cavalrymen. Gregg was in command of the Federal riders on the field, but because Custer became an American icon following his famous defeat and death at the Little Big Horn in 1876, it is his name that has become most prominent regarding the July 3 fight at East Cavalry Field.

Did Federal Army commander Maj. Gen. George G. Meade lose an opportunity to crush the Confederates by not counterattacking immediately after the repulse of Pickett's Charge?

WE WILL NEVER KNOW FOR CERTAIN, but the opportunity may not have been as golden as some would like to believe. Far from demoralized, there was still plenty of fight left in the Confederates after Pickett's Charge was beaten back. Only some 13,000 of Lee's remaining 60,000 or so troops (when one considers the Southern casualties to that point) participated in the charge, although they were spread out across several miles of front.

In the days and years afterward, Meade stated (in various ways) that he did not wish, by counterattacking, to suffer the type of defeat that he had just handed Robert E. Lee. Historians of course speculate and debate about how such a counterattack may have fared. It would have depended on many factors, including the number and type of troops Meade would have used to attack Lee's lines. It takes quite a bit of time to organize a large scale attack, and the men who had just beaten back the Confederate attack were exhausted, bloodied, and not organized for offensive action. They also would have needed additional ammunition and other supplies. A sizeable portion of one of Meade's corps, the VI Corps under Maj. Gen. John Sedgwick, had not seen much fighting during the battle and was quite fresh. Still, it would have taken time (perhaps hours) to bring that unit up and prepare it for an attack and then cross the mile of open terrain choked with bodies and debris in order to reach Confederate lines. (The VI Corps was the first large infantry organization sent to follow Lee on July 5 after the Southerners withdrew from the field.) By that time, it is reasonable to assume that Lee and his veteran officers would have arranged a defensive front capable of inflicting heavy losses on the Federals.

Federal and Confederate Quotes from the Gettysburg Campaign and Battle

Soldiers, politicians, and civilians left a wide variety of fascinating recollections about what they saw, heard, and thought about the wide-ranging, bloody, and decisive Gettysburg Campaign. Some of these quotes are well known and some less so, but each is worth reading and pondering in light of what occurred in Pennsylvania during those three critical summer days in 1863.

"Our army would be invincible if it could be properly organized and officered. There never were such men in an army before."

CONFEDERATE GEN. ROBERT E. LEE ON MAY 21, 1863,
AS HE PLANNED HIS CAMPAIGN INTO THE NORTH

"*The rascals are afraid we are going to overrun Pennsylvania. That would indeed be glorious, if we could ravage that state making her desolate like Virginia. It would be just punishment.*"

CONFEDERATE COLONEL CLEMENT A. EVANS OF THE 31ST GEORGIA INFANTRY, JUNE 4, 1863

"*Gen. Lee is venturing upon a very hazardous moment, and one that must be fruitless, if not disastrous.*"

CONFEDERATE MAJ. GEN. DANIEL H. HILL, WRITING TO HIS WIFE ON JUNE 25, 1863

"*The people look as sour as vinegar and, I have no doubt, would gladly send us all to Kingdom come if they could.*"

CONFEDERATE CORPS COMMANDER LT. GEN. RICHARD S. EWELL,
UPON ENTERING PENNSYLVANIA WITH HIS TROOPS

"*They will attack you in the morning and will come booming, skirmishers three deep. You will have to fight like the devil to hold your own.*"

FEDERAL CAVALRY DIVISION COMMANDER BRIG. GEN. JOHN BUFORD TO
COL. THOMAS DEVIN, ONE OF HIS BRIGADE COMMANDERS, ON THE NIGHT OF JUNE 30, 1863

"*None in the world.*"

CONFEDERATE CORPS COMMANDER AMBROSE P. HILL'S REPLY AFTER BEING ASKED BY
MAJ. GEN. HENRY HETH, ONE OF HILL'S DIVISION COMMANDERS, IF HE HAD ANY OBJECTION TO
HETH'S PLAN TO MARCH TO GETTYSBURG FROM CASHTOWN ON THE MORNING OF JULY 1, 1863

"*The Johnnies are coming! The Johnnies are coming!*"

FEDERAL PVT. THOMAS BENTON KELLY, 8TH ILLINOIS CAVALRY, AT 7:00 AM ON JULY 1, 1863,
AFTER SPOTTING THE CONFEDERATE ADVANCE ON GETTYSBURG ALONG THE CASHTOWN PIKE

"Forward, men, forward! For God's sake, forward!"

FEDERAL CORPS COMMANDER MAJ. GEN. JOHN F. REYNOLDS'
LAST WORDS BEFORE BEING MORTALLY WOUNDED WHILE LEADING THE IRON BRIGADE
INTO THE MORNING FIGHT AT HERBST'S WOODS ON JULY 1, 1863

"Well, I am not glad to see you by a damn sight, Doubleday."

CONFEDERATE BRIGADE COMMANDER BRIG. GEN. JOHN ARCHER
TO PRE-WAR ARMY COMRADE FEDERAL MAJ. GEN. ABNER DOUBLEDAY
AFTER BEING CAPTURED ON THE MORNING OF JULY 1, 1863

"I know how to fight; I have fit before."

SIXTY-NINE YEAR-OLD GETTYSBURG CITIZEN JOHN BURNS,
A SELF-PROCLAIMED VETERAN OF THE WAR OF 1812, AS HE VOLUNTEERED
TO JOIN THE FEDERALS FIGHTING WEST OF TOWN ON THE MORNING OF JULY 1, 1863

"We thought our last day had come."

GETTYSBURG BOY ALBERTUS MCCREARY, RECALLING THE TERROR AS HE AND HIS FAMILY
HID IN THEIR CELLAR WHILE THE BATTLE RAGED AROUND THEM ON JULY 1, 1863

*"Seventeenth, do your duty! Forward, double quick!
Charge bayonets!"*

LT. COL. DOUGLAS FOWLER, COMMANDING THE 17TH CONNECTICUT
ATOP BLOCHER'S KNOLL ON JULY 1, 1863, JUST MOMENTS BEFORE
A CONFEDERATE ARTILLERY ROUND SEVERED HIS HEAD FROM HIS BODY

*"It was a very hot day and I was in a hot place. My gun got
so hot I could scarcely hold to it. The bullets were thick as
hail . . . The men were falling every second but I paid
no attention to them. I could not help them."*

CORP. NATHAN COOPER, 151ST PENNSYLVANIA, WRITING
TO HIS WIFE ABOUT THE FIRST DAY OF BATTLE ON JULY 1, 1863

"The view presented astonished me, as the enemy was massed in my front, and extended to my right and left as far as I could see."

MAJ. GEN. LAFAYETTE MCLAWS, DIVISION COMMANDER IN LT. GEN. JAMES LONGSTREET'S CORPS, AFTER EXAMINING THE NEW FEDERAL LINE TO THE SOUTH ON JULY 2, 1863

"Fix bayonets, my brave Texans; forward and take those heights!"

MAJ. GEN. JOHN BELL HOOD, DIVISION COMMANDER IN LT. GEN. JAMES LONGSTREET'S CORPS, AT THE START OF THE JULY 2, 1863 ATTACK AGAINST THE FEDERAL LEFT

"You understand! Hold this ground at all costs!"

AN ORDER BY COL. STRONG VINCENT, COMMANDER OF A FEDERAL 5TH CORPS BRIGADE, TO COL. JOSHUA CHAMBERLAIN OF THE 20TH MAINE AS HE PLACED HIS REGIMENT ON THE EXTREME LEFT AT LITTLE ROUND TOP ON JULY 2, 1863

"Bayonet!"

COL. JOSHUA CHAMBERLAIN, COMMANDING 20TH MAINE, TO HIS MEN AS THEY FORMED TO COUNTERATTACK AND REPULSE THE CONFEDERATE ASSAULT ON THE SOUTHERN SLOPE OF LITTLE ROUND TOP ON JULY 2, 1863

"Colonel, I'll be damned if I don't think we are faced the wrong way; the rebs are up there in the woods behind us, on the right."

FEDERAL COLONEL JACOB SWEITZER'S FIFTH CORPS BRIGADE COLOR BEARER IN ROSE'S WHEATFIELD ON JULY 2, 1863, AS CONFEDERATES BEGIN TO NEARLY SURROUND THEIR POSITION

"Bullets were singing a 'double quick' march all around me."

CPL. OSCAR W. WEST, 32ND MASSACHUSETTS INFANTRY, RUNNING FROM THE CONFEDERATE ASSAULT ON ROSE'S WHEATFIELD ON JULY 2, 1863

"Clubs, knives, stones, fists — anything calculated to inflict death or pain was resorted to."

SGT. WILLIAM R. KIEFER OF THE 153RD PENNSYLVANIA INFANTRY, WRITING OF THE JULY 2, 1863, NIGHT ATTACK AGAINST EAST CEMETERY HILL BY TWO BRIGADES OF CONFEDERATES FROM MAJ. GEN. JUBAL A. EARLY'S DIVISION

"It is all right now, it is all right now."

FEDERAL ARMY COMMANDER MAJ. GEN. GEORGE G. MEADE ON THE EVENING OF JULY 2, 1863, AFTER HIS ARMY HAD SUCCESSFULLY REPULSED EVERY CONFEDERATE ATTACK AGAINST MANY PARTS OF HIS EXTENDED LINE

"I think the people of this place are very kind considering we came here to kill off their husbands and sons."

CONFEDERATE SOLDIER ON JULY 2, 1863, TALKING ABOUT THE KIND TREATMENT OF THE REBEL WOUNDED PROVIDED BY GETTYSBURG'S RESIDENTS

"I ordered artillery from wherever I could find it, where I thought it could be spared, without any regard to the commands of others, except to inform them that it was necessary."

FEDERAL ARMY ARTILLERY COMMANDER BRIG. GEN. HENRY HUNT, RECALLING HOW HE SET UP A STRONG LINE OF ARTILLERY ON THE MORNING OF JULY 3, 1863, IN ANTICIPATION OF A CONFEDERATE ASSAULT AGAINST THE UNION CENTER

"General . . . it is my opinion that no fifteen thousand men ever arrayed for battle can take that position."

CONFEDERATE CORPS COMMANDER LT. GEN. JAMES LONGSTREET'S RECOLLECTION OF THE ADVICE HE GAVE GEN. ROBERT E. LEE DURING PREPARATIONS FOR PICKETT'S CHARGE ON JULY 3, 1863

"The enemy is there, and I will strike him there."

GEN. ROBERT E. LEE TO LT. GEN. JAMES LONGSTREET, CONFIRMING THAT THE JULY 3, 1863 ATTACK WILL GO FORWARD

"It is not as hard to get there as it looks. I was there yesterday with my brigade. The real difficulty is to stay there after you get there — for the whole infernal Yankee army is up there in a bunch!"

CONFEDERATE BRIGADE COMMANDER BRIG. GEN. AMBROSE R. WRIGHT TO COL. E. PORTER ALEXANDER AS THE TWO OFFICERS EXAMINED THE FOCAL POINT OF THE JULY 3, 1863, ATTACK AGAINST THE FEDERAL CENTER

"If you are to advance at all you must come at once or we will not be able to support you as we ought, but the enemy's fire has not slackened materially and there are still at least 18 guns firing from the Cemetery."

COL. E. PORTER ALEXANDER, ONE OF LT. GEN. JAMES LONGSTREET'S ARTILLERY COMMANDERS, IN A NOTE TO MAJ. GEN. GEORGE E. PICKETT TO COMMENCE HIS INFANTRY ATTACK ON JULY 3, 1863

"General, shall I advance?"

MAJ. GEN. GEORGE E. PICKETT, ASKING LT. GEN. JAMES LONGSTREET FOR THE ORDER TO BEGIN WHAT WOULD BECOME KNOWN AS PICKETT'S CHARGE ON JULY 3, 1863; UNABLE TO SPEAK, LONGSTREET NODDED HIS APPROVAL

"Up, men, and to your posts! Don't forget today that you are from Old Virginia!"

MAJ. GEN. GEORGE PICKETT EXHORTING HIS MEN AS THEY PREPARED TO CHARGE ON JULY 3, 1863

"This is going to be a heller! Prepare for the worst!"

CONFEDERATE SOLDIER IN PICKETT'S DIVISION TO HIS COMRADES AS THEY STEPPED OFF TOWARD THE FEDERAL POSITION ON THE AFTERNOON OF JULY 3, 1863

*"Oh, if I could just come out of this charge
safely how thankful would I be!"*

LT. JOHN DOOLEY, 1ST VIRGINIA INFANTRY OF PICKETT'S DIVISION,
JUST BEFORE PICKETT'S CHARGE ON JULY 3, 1863

---

*"At once they were enveloped in a dense cloud of
smoke and dust. Arms, heads, blankets, guns and
knapsacks were thrown and tossed to the clear air."*

LT. COL. FRANKLIN SAWYER, 8TH OHIO INFANTRY, WRITING ABOUT THE EFFECT OF FEDERAL
ARTILLERY ON THE ADVANCING CONFEDERATE SOLDIERS DURING PICKETT'S CHARGE ON JULY 3, 1863

---

*"A perfect mangled mass of flesh and blood,
indistinguishable one from the other."*

CAPT. BENJAMIN FARINHOLT, 53RD VIRGINIA INFANTRY, DESCRIBING THE
RESULT OF ONE FEDERAL ARTILLERY SHELL THAT KILLED THIRTEEN OF HIS
FELLOW CONFEDERATES DURING PICKETT'S CHARGE ON JULY 3, 1863

---

*"Do not hurry, men, and fire too fast — let them come up
close before you fire, and then aim low, and steadily."*

FEDERAL DIVISION COMMANDER BRIG. GEN. JOHN GIBBON TO HIS MEN ON JULY 3, 1863,
AS THEY WAITED BEHIND A LOW STONE WALL FOR THE APPROACHING CONFEDERATES

---

*"We bowled them over like nine pins. . . . In two minutes there
were only groups of two or three men running round wildly, like
chickens with their heads off. We were cheering like mad."*

CAPT. HENRY ABBOTT, 20TH MASSACHUSETTS INFANTRY, DESCRIBING THE DEVASTATION
SUFFERED BY THE CONFEDERATES ATTACKING SOUTH OF THE COPSE OF TREES ON JULY 3, 1863

"General Pickett, place your division in rear of this hill and be ready to repel the advance of the enemy should they follow up their advantage."

GEN. ROBERT E. LEE TO MAJ. GEN. GEORGE PICKETT AS SURVIVORS AND WOUNDED STREAMED BACK FROM THE JULY 3, 1863 ASSAULT THAT WOULD FOREVERMORE BEAR PICKETT'S NAME

"General Lee, I have no division now."

MAJ. GEN. GEORGE E. PICKETT TO GEN. ROBERT E. LEE, AFTER THE REPULSE OF THE INFANTRY ATTACK ON JULY 3, 1863

"As many of our poor wounded as possible must be taken home."

GEN. ROBERT E. LEE, PLANNING HIS ARMY'S RETREAT FROM GETTYSBURG FOLLOWING THE FAILURE OF PICKETT'S CHARGE ON JULY 3, 1863

"It means that Uncle Robert has got a hell of a whipping."

CONFEDERATE SOLDIER ON JULY 5, 1863 RESPONDING TO A CITIZEN'S INQUIRY AS TO THE REASON WHY ALL THE SOUTHERN SOLDIERS WERE RETREATING FROM THE BATTLEFIELD

"I hope we will never cross the Potomac again, for I don't believe we ever made anything by crossing it yet."

PVT. W.G. THOMPSON, 13TH NORTH CAROLINA INFANTRY, IN A LETTER HOME ON JULY 14, 1863, AFTER THE CONFEDERATES FINALLY MADE IT TO SAFETY ACROSS THE POTOMAC

"We had them in our grasp. We had only to stretch forth our hands and they were ours. And nothing I could say or do could make the Army move."

PRESIDENT ABRAHAM LINCOLN ON JULY 14, 1863, FRUSTRATED THAT MAJ. GEN. GEORGE G. MEADE HAD NOT ATTACKED THE CONFEDERATES BEFORE THEY ESCAPED ACROSS THE POTOMAC RIVER

The Road to Gettysburg

The American Civil War was two years old in May of 1863. Although the Confederacy had suffered several significant setbacks in the Western Theater, Robert E. Lee's Army of Northern Virginia established an impressive string of victories against its Federal opponents in the East. Lee's success began against the Army of the Potomac in June 1862 outside the gates of Richmond in the Seven Days' Battles, and continued farther north that August at Second Manassas. Although Lee's Maryland Campaign stalled at Antietam (Sharpsburg) in September, he defeated the Federals soundly at Fredericksburg in December and once more at Chancellorsville in May 1863. After losing corps commander Lt. Gen. Thomas J. "Stonewall" Jackson in the latter campaign, Lee reorganized his army from two corps to three. Lt. Gen. James Longstreet retained command of his First Corps, and Lt. Gens. Richard S. Ewell and Ambrose P. Hill were placed in command of the Second and Third Corps, respectively.

Lee determined to shift hostilities out of war-torn Virginia and onto Northern soil. His general plan was to operate in enemy territory as long as possible and, when opportunity presented itself, meet portions of the Federal army in Pennsylvania and defeat each in detail. If he moved north and threatened major northern cities such as Washington, Baltimore, Harrisburg, or Philadelphia, he could draw the Federals to him like prey to a spider's web. Lee knew he was running an enormous risk by exposing the Southern capital at Richmond and moving so far from his base of supplies, but he believed a decisive victory on enemy soil might convince the North to end the war and grant the Confederacy its independence.

The photograph above, taken by Timothy O'Sullivan on June 3, 1863, has been recently identified as the first recorded image of the Gettysburg Campaign. Here, Federal army pontoon bridges span the Rappahannock River near Fredericksburg at the "Lower Crossing." The view looks west toward the Confederate position on the heights in the background. Pontoon bridges were constructed by lashing pontoon boats together in a line from shore to shore laying boards on top to create a surface over which troops could march and wagons and artillery could roll.

The map on the opposite page shows the march routes of the various units of both armies through northern Virginia, Maryland, and Pennsylvania. Richard Ewell's Corps led the Confederate army as it swung west and then north toward Culpepper Court House and then into the Shenandoah Valley, with James Longstreet's Corps marching next in order. A. P. Hill's Corps, which Lee left in place opposite Fredericksburg to divert attention from his initial movement toward the Valley, followed Ewell and Longstreet on June 10.

From June 9 through the start of the Gettysburg battle on July 1, opposing cavalry and infantry fought several skirmishes and pitched battles, including Brandy Station, Second Winchester, Stephenson's Depot, Aldie, Middleburg, Upperville, and many more. The marches were long, difficult, and exhausting. No one knew where the fluid campaign would take them or what, exactly, Lee hoped to achieve once north of the Mason Dixon Line.

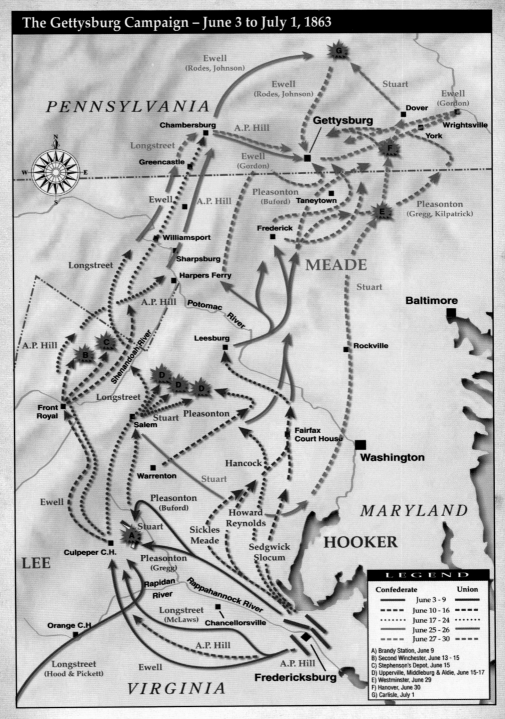

The Gettysburg Campaign – June 3 to July 1, 1863

PENNSYLVANIA

Ewell
(Rodes, Johnson)

Ewell
(Rodes, Johnson)

Stuart

G

Ewell
(Gordon)

Dover

Gettysburg

Chambersburg

A.P. Hill

Ewell
(Gordon)

Wrightsville

York

F

Longstreet

Greencastle

Ewell

A.P. Hill

Pleasonton
(Buford)

Taneytown

Pleasonton
(Gregg, Kilpatrick)

Williamsport

E

Sharpsburg

Frederick

MEADE

Longstreet

Harpers Ferry

A.P. Hill

Potomac   River

Stuart

Baltimore

A.P. Hill

Leesburg

C

Shenandoah River

Rockville

B

D

D   D

Longstreet

Front
Royal

Stuart

Pleasonton

Fairfax
Court House

Salem

Washington

Hancock

Warrenton

Stuart

MARYLAND

Ewell

Pleasonton
(Buford)

A

Howard
Reynolds

HOOKER

Stuart

Sickles
Meade

Sedgwick
Slocum

Culpeper C.H.

LEE

Pleasonton
(Gregg)

LEGEND

Rapidan
River

Rappahannock River

Confederate   Union
                    June 3 - 9
                    June 10 - 16
Longstreet
(McLaws)   Chancellorsville   June 17 - 24
                    June 25 - 26
Orange C.H.   June 27 - 30

A.P. Hill
A) Brandy Station, June 9
B) Second Winchester, June 13 - 15
Longstreet
(Hood & Pickett)   Ewell   A.P. Hill   C) Stephenson's Depot, June 15
                                        D) Upperville, Middleburg & Aldie, June 15-17
                                        E) Westminster, June 29
VIRGINIA   Fredericksburg   F) Hanover, June 30
                                        G) Carlisle, July 1

Before Lee's army began its march north, the largest and bloodiest cavalry battle that would ever take place in North America unfolded on the rolling plains near Brandy Station, Virginia, on June 9, 1863 (above). Federal cavalry commanded by Brig. Gen. Alfred Pleasonton crossed the Rappahannock River early that morning to surprise and engage the Confederate cavalry under the vainglorious but skilled Maj. Gen. James Ewell Brown Stuart. Nearly 20,000 cavalrymen fought fitfully for fourteen hours (as represented below in a *Harper's Weekly* engraving) resulting in more than 1,400 combined casualties and delaying Lee's march north by one full day. Most significant, Union cavalry had finally come of age.

As the three Confederate corps marched north through the Shenandoah Valley toward Maryland, Stuart's troopers screened the infantry by defending the mountain

(LIBRARY OF CONGRESS)

passes to the east to keep the Federal horsemen from tracking it. When the Federal troopers tried to break Stuart's screen, pitched cavalry battles erupted near Virginia towns such as Aldie (above), Middleburg, and Upperville (below). Stuart was nearly defeated at the last fight, but the Union riders were kept at bay. Lee's infantry was able to advance north virtually unmolested.

After the fights for the mountain passes, J.E.B. Stuart proposed a bold plan to Lee: make a ride around the Union army with his cavalry to get between the Federals and Washington, D.C., so he could threaten that city and others important to the North and cause havoc and panic in the Federal capital as Lee advanced into Pennsylvania. (Stuart had made a similar though shorter ride the previous year.)

(LIBRARY OF CONGRESS)

When Lee approved, Stuart gathered just over one-half of his cavalry, rode east toward Washington, and then moved north to link up with the Southern army once in Pennsylvania. Once Stuart left on his ride, General Lee lost contact with his cavalry commander—the eyes and ears of his army.

Stuart's grand plan went awry almost from the start. After a skirmish with Federal cavalry at Fairfax Court House, Virginia, he bogged down his column by capturing 125 Federal wagons at Rockville, Maryland. Stuart ran into more Federal cavalry at Westminster, Maryland on June 29, where a small contingent of only 108 troopers of the 1st Delaware Cavalry attacked him in the town's streets (shown above in a period

photograph). Stuart captured nearly the whole lot, but it delayed his march by more than half a day.

Stuart, meanwhile, his men and animals growing weaker by the day, expended a significant amount of time trying to find the marching Confederate army in Pennsylvania. He became further frustrated when on June 30 a Federal cavalry division under Brig. Gen. H. Judson Kilpatrick attacked the Southern troopers and a full-scale battle raged in and around the town of Hanover. The fight cost Stuart another entire day and forced him further east. The monument to the left commemorates the Hanover fight, the first large battle on Pennsylvania soil during the campaign.

Confederate infantry in Lt. Gen. Richard S. Ewell's Second Corps crossed into Pennsylvania on June 23. One of his divisions passed through Gettysburg on June 26, while the other two marched west of Gettysburg toward the state capital at Harrisburg. To answer this "invasion" of Pennsylvania by Rebel troops, Pennsylvania's Governor Andrew G. Curtin sent up a call for volunteer militia to rally to arms. Posters such as the one to the right were put up anywhere people would see them. Many citizens loaded their valuables and livestock and sent them east of the Susquehanna River into protective hiding, and thousands of able-bodied men of all ages volunteered to fight.

THE ENEMY IS APPROACHING!

I MUST RELY UPON THE PEOPLE FOR THE

DEFENCE of the STATE!

AND HAVE Called THE MILITIA for that PURPOSE!

A. G. CURTIN, Governor of Pennsylvania.

THE TERM OF SERVICE WILL ONLY BE WHILE THE DANGER OF THE STATE IS IMMINENT.

One such unit was the 26th Pennsylvania Emergency Militia, made up of farmers, laborers, shopkeepers, and college students. One company was comprised of students from Gettysburg. They were sent back there on June 26 to defend the mountain passes to the west and southwest. The 26th's nearly 750 men joined with a local volunteer cavalry group raised by Gettysburg resident Robert Bell and marched west on the road leading to Cashtown. About four miles from town, Lt. Col. Elijah V. White's cavalry battalion, part of Ewell's Corps, attacked and scattered the green militia and troopers. By the end of the day, nearly one-third of the militia were prisoners and stripped of their shiny new guns and new shoes. The following day Early marched toward Harrisburg, and Gettysburg residents hoped they had seen the worst that the war would bring to them.

To commemorate their service at Gettysburg, veterans of the 26th Pennsylvania Emergency Militia erected a monument (right) in 1892 at the spot the Cashtown Pike enters Gettysburg. The young boy, seemingly fresh from the farm field, displays a bit more defiance than his comrades were able to muster on June 26, 1863.

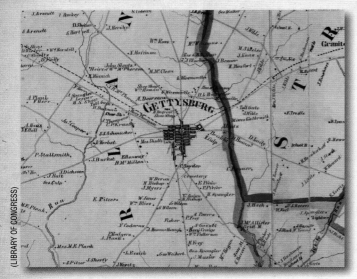

The 1858 map at left shows the extensive road network leading to Gettysburg that eventually drew both armies to the town on July 1, 1863. Following his fight at Hanover on June 30, J.E.B. Stuart dragged his exhausted cavalrymen farther north to Carlisle, where he held the town under siege. A brigade of A. P. Hill's Corps commanded by Brig. Gen. J. Johnston Pettigrew marched his troops from their camps at Cashtown seven miles east to Gettysburg to look for supplies. What he found instead was Federal cavalry approaching the town from the south (which turned out to be veteran troopers of Brig. Gen. John Buford's division). Pettigrew retraced his steps and reported the news to his superiors. The news seemed to confirm intelligence that elements of the Federal army were much closer to south-central Pennsylvania than Robert E. Lee expected. Pettigrew's immediate superiors, however, discounted his report.

That day, June 30, 1863, two of Lee's corps – those of Lt. Gen. James Longstreet and A.P. Hill – were at Chambersburg and Cashtown west of Gettysburg. The third corps under Richard Ewell was threatening Harrisburg. Lee had still not heard from his chief cavalryman, J.E.B. Stuart, and the army commander sorely missed his reconnaissance and information-gathering skills.

General Buford rode through the town with his two brigades and examined the ridges and hills to the west and north. Locals and his own troopers informed him that the bulk of Lee's army was in those directions, and Buford predicted that he would be attacked in the morning (July 1) along the roads leading to Gettysburg like the spokes of a wheel. If he could mount a defense on those ridges long enough for supporting Federal infantry marching up from the south behind him to arrive, perhaps Lee could be drawn into a battle on ground advantageous to the Federal army. Buford placed outposts of his men along the ridges to watch every approach into town.

Confederate infantry felt confident of success as the sun sank below the horizon on June 30. J.E.B. Stuart kept riding north searching for word about the army's whereabouts, and Federal infantry just south of the border in Maryland wondered if more bad tidings awaited them on yet another battlefield.

Buford's troopers, meanwhile, watched and waited.

Wednesday, July 1, 1863

As the sun arose on the morning of Wednesday, July 1, 1863, approximately 7,500 Confederates of Maj. Gen. Henry Heth's Division began marching from their camp near Cashtown to Gettysburg seven miles to the east. If there were Federals at Gettysburg, as Brig. Gen. Johnston Pettigrew reported the previous day, Heth expected nothing more than militia, which his veteran infantry would dispatch with ease. The division commander would regret his mistake.

Waiting for the approaching Confederates were dismounted cavalry outposts sprinkled along the elaborate network placed by Brig. Gen. John Buford to watch the roads entering Gettysburg from the west, north, and east. When Southerners marching at the head of Heth's column reached a small bridge spanning Marsh Creek about half the distance to the town, they spotted the blue troopers posted atop Knoxlyn Ridge. Some thought they belonged to Lt. Gen. James Longstreet's Confederate Corps. Heth suspected they were Pennsylvania militia—the troops Pettigrew had seen—and spread out a skirmish line on both sides of the Chambersburg Pike.

Within moments a shot from the ridge ahead shattered the morning calm. Heth's skirmishers tightened their grips on their rifled muskets and his artillery crews readied one of the guns.

Although no one yet knew it, the Battle of Gettysburg had begun.

At the home of Ephraim Wisler (above) along the
Chambersburg Pike atop Knoxlyn Ridge, Lt. Marcellus
E. Jones of the 8th Illinois Cavalry fired the first shot at
Heth's Confederates about 7:30 a.m. to open the battle.
Heth's skirmishers replied with shots of their own and unlimbered one cannon that
opened on the dismounted troopers along the ridge here. Decades later, Jones
traveled to the spot with several comrades to place a small memorial (inset above right)
to forever mark the location from which he fired his "first shot."

John Buford, in command of the two brigades of Federal cavalry that met Heth's Confederate advance on Gettysburg that first morning, placed his main battle line atop McPherson's Ridge, about one mile east of Knoxlyn Ridge and closer to town. Outnumbered nearly five-to-one, Buford deftly held back the enemy infantry for two hours until Federal infantry commanded by Maj. Gen. John F. Reynolds arrived to support him. To memorialize the stand made by the reserved yet tough-as-nails Buford, a group of admirers and former comrades placed his statue (left) atop the ridge in 1895. The panorama below faces east from the ridge, looking back toward Gettysburg and displays a large swath of the initial battlefield of the first day. To the right of Buford's statue stands the monument for Capt. James A. Hall's Maine artillery, which fought desperately here, and the equestrian statue of General Reynolds.

July 1 - 9:30 to 11:15 a.m.: The Fight for McPherson's Ridge

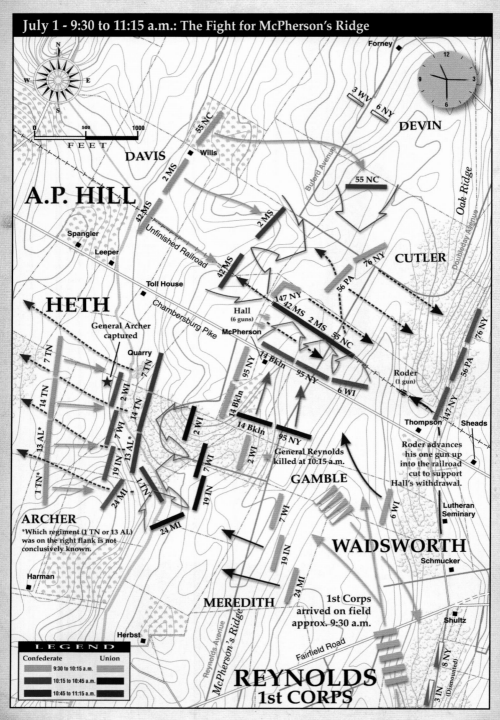

Forney

3 WV

6 NY

DEVIN

N
W E
S

FEET
0   500   1000

55 NC

Wills

DAVIS

2 MS

42 MS

A.P. HILL

55 NC

Oak Ridge

Spangler

Unfinished Railroad

Leeper

2 MS

42 MS

Buford Avenue

Doubleday Avenue

CUTLER

76 NY

56 PA

Toll House

Chambersburg Pike

147 NY

42 MS   2 MS

55 NC

76 NY

HETH

General Archer captured

Quarry

Hall
(6 guns)

McPherson

56 PA

7 TN

14 TN

2 WI

7 TN

14 TN

13 AL*

19 IN

7 WI

13 AL*

1 TN*

24 MI

1 TN

14 Bkln

95 NY

95 NY

6 WI

Roder
(1 gun)

147 NY

Thompson

Sheads

Roder advances
his one gun up
into the railroad
cut to support
Hall's withdrawal.

14 Bkln

14 Bkln

2 WI

2 WI

95 NY

General Reynolds
killed at 10:15 a.m.

GAMBLE

7 WI

6 WI

Lutheran
Seminary

ARCHER

*Which regiment (1 TN or 13 AL)
was on the right flank is not
conclusively known.

19 IN

7 WI

24 MI

WADSWORTH

Schmucker

Harman

19 IN

24 MI

Herbst

MEREDITH

1st Corps
arrived on field
approx. 9:30 a.m.

Shultz

McPherson's Ridge

Reynolds Avenue

Fairfield Road

3 IN

8 NY
(Dismounted)

REYNOLDS
1st CORPS

LEGEND

Confederate	Union
9:30 to 10:15 a.m.	
10:15 to 10:45 a.m.	
10:45 to 11:15 a.m.	

(LIBRARY OF CONGRESS)

Buford used the cupola of the Lutheran Theological Seminary (above) as an observation post to watch the initial fighting west of town. Standing just a few hundred yards east of McPherson's Ridge, the same cupola was later used by Confederates when they pushed the Federals into and beyond Gettysburg. By mid-morning both sides had fed thousands of men into the fighting along McPherson's Ridge, enlarging an already significant engagement into a considerable contest for the heights west of Gettysburg (see map on opposite facing page). General Reynolds was shot and killed while leading elements of his own Federal I Corps into the spreading battle. He was the highest-ranking officer on either side to lose his life at Gettysburg. A simple wooden sign tacked to a nearby tree (right) marked the spot of his mortal wounding. It was later memorialized permanently with a stone monument that is a favorite of battlefield visitors today.

(LIBRARY OF CONGRESS)

By late morning the heavy fighting north and south of the Chambersburg Pike along McPherson's Ridge included two of General Heth's Confederate divisions against Reynolds' troops. North of the pike, Brig. Gen. Joseph Davis' Southerners battled the Federals of Brig. Gen. Lysander Cutler's brigade. South of the pike, a Confederate brigade under Brig. Gen. James A. Archer was feeling the weight of the advance of the Federal "Iron Brigade" commanded by Brig. Gen. Solomon Meredith.

That morning, one of Gettysburg's oldest citizens, 69-year-old John Burns, walked out of his Chambersburg Street home and joined the Federals in the fight, the only citizen known to have done so during the battle. Burns (below left) was wounded at least three times during his fight against Archer's Brigade. A sergeant in the 7th Wisconsin Infantry described the old curmudgeon as "true blue and grit to the backbone." After spending the night lying on the field, he made his way to the home of a friend and recuperated. After the battle he enjoyed posing with his ancient flintlock musket and telling his story to anyone who would listen. President Lincoln spent time with Burns during his visit for the dedication of the Soldiers' National Cemetery in November 1863. In memory of the old patriot citizen who took up arms and fought to defend his home, the Pennsylvania General Assembly dedicated the statue of Burns (below) on July 1, 1903 on McPherson's Ridge.

Running east to west and cutting through the ridges west of Gettysburg in the middle of the first day's battlefield ran an unfinished railroad bed. Many of General Davis' Confederates jumped into it, thinking it

would provide cover and protection. Its apparent strength as a defensive position was deceiving, and its depth and steep sides turned a place of refuge into a death trap when Federals lined the top and fired into it. Large numbers of Confederates were killed or wounded there, and many more were captured. The Alfred Waud drawing (above) produced shortly after the battle exaggerates the depth of the railroad cut, but as can be seen in the photo below, the banks were steep in several areas.

July 1 - 2:30 to 3:40 p.m.: Rodes Attacks Oak Ridge

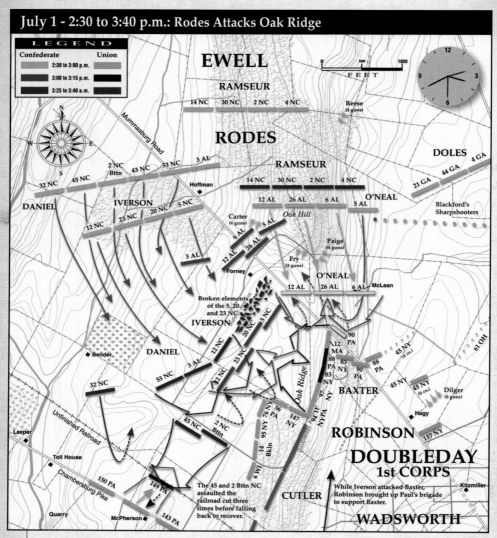

LEGEND

Confederate	Union
2:30 to 3:00 p.m.	
3:00 to 3:15 p.m.	
3:25 to 3:40 a.m.	

EWELL

RAMSEUR

14 NC 30 NC 2 NC 4 NC

Reese (4 guns)

RODES

2 NC Bttn 43 NC 53 NC 3 AL

RAMSEUR

14 NC 30 NC 2 NC 4 NC

DOLES

21 GA 44 GA 4 GA

32 NC 45 NC

Hoffman

IVERSON

23 NC 20 NC 5 NC

12 AL 26 AL 6 AL

O'NEAL

5 AL

Blackford's Sharpshooters

DANIEL

12 NC

Carter (4 guns)

Oak Hill

5 AL

3 AL

6 AL

12 AL 26 AL

Paige (4 guns)

Fry (4 guns)

Forney

O'NEAL

12 AL 26 AL 6 AL McLean

Broken elements of the 5, 20, and 23 NC.

IVERSON

20 NC 5 NC

12 NC 23 NC 3 AL

Oak Ridge

90 PA

12 MA

88 PA 83 NY 90 PA

88 PA

83 NY

45 NY (4 co.)

45 NY

Bender

DANIEL

53 NC

BAXTER

45 NY (6 co.)

Dilger (6 guns)

32 NC

45 NC

2 NC Bttn

95 NY 76 NY

56 PA 147 NY

94 NY 11 NY

97 NY

Hágy

157 NY

Leeper

Unfinished Railroad

14 Bkln

6 WI

ROBINSON

DOUBLEDAY
1st CORPS

Toll House

Chambersburg Pike

150 PA

149 PA

The 45 and 2 Bttn NC assaulted the railroad cut three times before falling back to recover.

CUTLER

While Iverson attacked Baxter, Robinson brought up Paul's brigade to support Baxter.

Kitzmiller

Quarry

McPherson

143 PA

WADSWORTH

Both sides took advantage of a noontime lull in the fighting west of town to regroup. The respite didn't last long. Maj. Gen. Robert E. Rodes, commander of a division in the Confederate corps of Lt. Gen. Richard S. Ewell, arrived on the field from the north and launched a disjointed attack on the Federal line from his position on Oak Hill. Shoddy reconnaissance and poor planning decimated Alfred Iverson's Southern brigade when Brig. Gen. Henry Baxter's Federals rose from behind a stone wall and fired a volley at point blank range. Scores of North Carolinians died as they marched—in a nearly perfect line—and many more were wounded and captured. The Southern dead were buried after the battle in long trench graves, forevermore referred to as "Iverson's Pits."

Dedicated at the 75th Anniversary of the battle in 1938 by President Franklin D. Roosevelt, the Eternal Peace Light Memorial (above) honors the soldiers of both North and South. A flame at the top, symbolic of the peace that has reigned since the end of the war, burns day and night. The vista from the monument's front steps affords a view of the ground over which Rodes' Confederate division attacked the Federals of Brig. Gen. John Robinson's division along Oak Ridge, as well as much of the first day's battlefield farther south near the Railroad Cut and the town of Gettysburg.

One of the battlefield's most uniquely shaped monuments is that of the 90th Pennsylvania Infantry (right) of Baxter's brigade, which stands along Oak Ridge. The granite memorial is in the shape of a tree trunk, and features a bird's nest near the top. One story of the regiment's fight claims a nest was knocked from a tree during the battle here, and amidst a hail of bullets and shell, one of the Pennsylvanians picked it up and returned it to the tree.

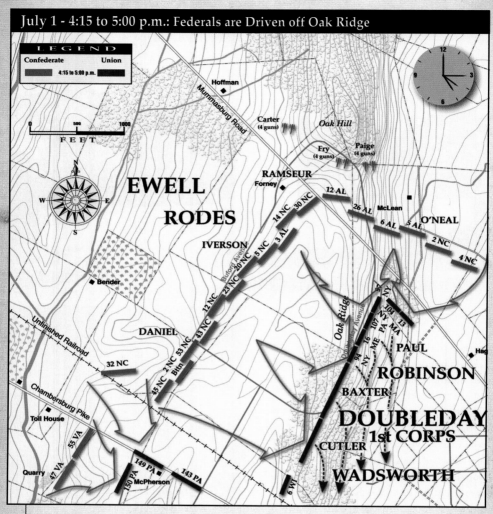

July 1 - 4:15 to 5:00 p.m.: Federals are Driven off Oak Ridge

By about 5:00 p.m., the line on Oak Ridge manned by Robinson's division (plus the brigade of Brig. Lysander Cutler to Robinson's left, about 4,000 soldiers in all) had become untenable. Rodes' veterans pounded the Federal position from the north and west with some 6,000 men. Unable to hold, Robinson's and Cutler's men retreated southeast toward Seminary Ridge.

Farther south, Maj. Gen. Abner Doubleday's outnumbered division (commanded by Brig. Gen. Thomas Rowley when Doubleday took command upon Reynolds' death) fighting atop McPherson's Ridge also began to give way under the weight of Heth's attack. Within a short time the Confederates would claim the heights west of Gettysburg.

The photo above was taken prior to 1904 by Gettysburg's Mumper Studios and depicts Oak Ridge just south of the Mummasburg Road. The camera faces south, with Robinson Avenue running left-right, and Doubleday Avenue proceeding off into the distance. Doubleday Avenue approximates the line held along the stone wall here by the regiments of Brig. Gen. John Robinson's division. The Confederates of Maj. Gen. Robert E. Rodes' Division attacked the Federals from the right on the afternoon of July 1. On the far right is the monument of the 88th Pennsylvania Infantry, dedicated in 1889. It was from that line that the Pennsylvanians helped repulse the attack of Iverson's Confederate brigade and captured two Southern flags.

Out of sight to the right of the photo, in the field over which Iverson's men attacked, stands a small stone memorial placed by the veterans of the 88th Pennsylvania about six years prior to the dedication of their main monument. The stone marks the furthest point at which the Pennsylvanians left the cover of the stone wall and counterattacked the 20th and 23rd North Carolina regiments. By the time their fight here was over, the Pennsylvanians lost one-fourth of their men.

In the distance is the impressive 51-foot high shaft of the 83rd New York Infantry's monument, placed in 1888. At its top is a bronze eagle with a wing span of nearly six feet. At the bottom is the regiment's motto "Ratione Aut Vi," which means "By Reason or Force." That day, the New Yorkers helped repulse Rodes' initial attack, but the Federal line ultimately gave way against superior numbers of equally determined Confederates.

The William Tipton photo above, taken about 1900, looks northwest from Blocher's Knoll. During the afternoon of July 1, Brig. Gen. Francis C. Barlow moved his XI Corps Federal division forward from his position near the County Almshouse to the knoll (see map on opposite facing page). There, his men were attacked by Maj. Gen. Jubal Early's Confederate division and surrounded, suffering horrible losses. Col. Douglas Fowler, the commander of the 7th Connecticut Infantry (the regiment's monument is shown in the photo) was decapitated by a Confederate artillery shell.

Below is a detail from the massive mural painted on a postwar building depicting a desperate rearguard action by Federals of Col. Charles Coster's XI Corps brigade as they covered the withdrawal of Barlow's survivors (see bottom of map). Coster's position was also overrun by Early's men, and the XI Corps was pushed into and through Gettysburg in a massive rout.

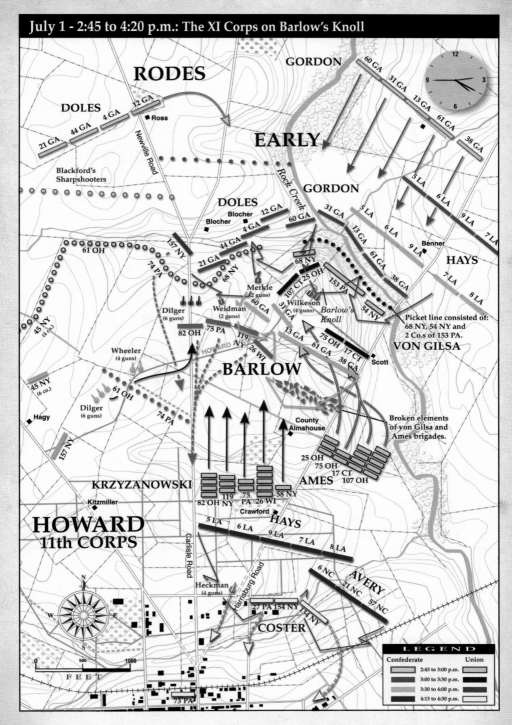

July 1 - 2:45 to 4:20 p.m.: The XI Corps on Barlow's Knoll

RODES

DOLES

21 GA   44 GA   4 GA   12 GA

Ross

Blackford's
Sharpshooters

Newville Road

GORDON

60 GA   31 GA   13 GA   61 GA   38 GA

EARLY

Rock Creek

GORDON

5 LA   6 LA   9 LA   7 LA

HAYS

Benner

DOLES

Blocher   Blocher   12 GA   60 GA

Blocher   4 GA

44 GA   21 GA   68 NY

157 NY

74 PA

61 OH

45 NY
(4 co.)

Dilger
(6 guns)

Merkle
(2 guns)

Weidman
(2 guns)   60 GA   31 GA

68 NY

31 GA   5 LA   6 LA   9 LA   7 LA

13 GA   61 GA   38 GA

8 LA

68 NY

107 CT 25 OH

Wilkeson
(4 guns)   153 PA   7 LA   8 LA

Barlow's
Knoll   54 NY

Picket line consisted of:
68 NY, 54 NY and
2 Cos.s of 153 PA.

VON GILSA

Wheeler
(4 guns)

82 OH   75 PA   119
NY   26 WI

13 GA   75 NY   17 CT

61 GA   38 GA

Scott

45 NY
(6 co.)

61 OH

Dilger
(6 guns)   74 PA

BARLOW

Broken elements
of von Gilsa and
Ames brigades.

157 NY

Hagy

County
Almshouse

25 OH
75 OH   17 CT
107 OH

KRZYZANOWSKI

119
82 OH NY   75
PA   26 WI   58 NY

AMES

Kitzmiller

Crawford

HOWARD
11th CORPS

Carlisle Road

5 LA   6 LA   9 LA   7 LA

HAYS

8 LA

Heckman
(4 guns)

Hartsburg Road

6 NC
21 NC   57 NC

AVERY

N

W   E

S

27 PA 154 NY 134 NY

COSTER

0   500   1000

FEET

73 PA

LEGEND

Confederate	Union
2:45 to 3:00 p.m.	
3:00 to 3:30 p.m.	
3:30 to 4:00 p.m.	
4:15 to 4:30 p.m.	

59

July 1 - 3:15 to 4:30 a.m.: The Final Push on McPherson's Ridge

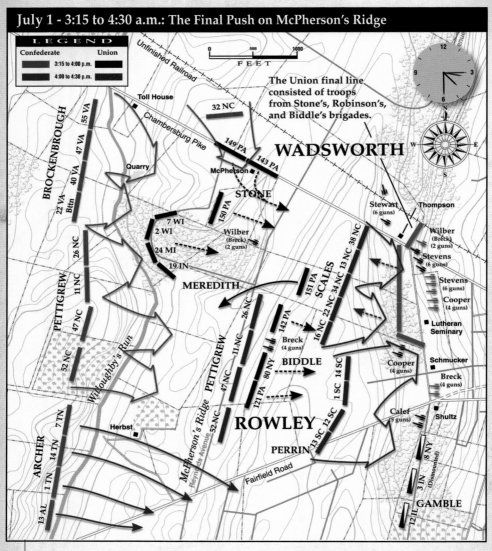

LEGEND

Confederate — 3:15 to 4:00 p.m.
Confederate — 4:00 to 4:30 p.m.
Union — 3:15 to 4:00 p.m.
Union — 4:00 to 4:30 p.m.

The Union final line consisted of troops from Stone's, Robinson's, and Biddle's brigades.

As the Confederates, who enjoyed a nearly two-to-one advantage on the battlefield, pushed the Federal XI Corps off the heights north of town, they likewise drove back the I Corps from McPherson's Ridge (see map above). Regiments of General Doubleday's division (under General Rowley) and General Meredith's division made a final determined stand along Seminary Ridge with Federal artillery in support. They were unable, however, to hold out for long. After trying to hold back the Southerners for a half hour, the Federal line at the Seminary cracked, sending the I Corps soldiers east toward the town.

Col. William Gamble's Federal cavalry brigade lent assistance to the infantry's left flank, but after more than a half hour of intense fighting, brigades in Lt. Gen. Ambrose P. Hill's Third Corps led by Gens. James Archer and Johnston Pettigrew and Col. John Brockenbrough broke the Federal line along Seminary Ridge. The monument of the 7th Wisconsin Infantry of the Federal Iron Brigade of the I Corps (left) stands as a testament to the heavy losses (nearly 50%) it suffered on July 1.

Caught in the middle of the first day's fighting west of town was the home of widow Mary Thompson (below). General Robert E. Lee, who pitched his headquarters tents in an orchard just south of the home after his Southerners gained this ground, may have taken some meals inside Thompson's home.

61

(LIBRARY OF CONGRESS)

Routed from the ridges and knolls west and north of town, the Federal I and XI Corps, together with artillery and cavalry, streamed east and south through the town and fields to seek cover on a new defensive position established atop Cemetery Hill to the southeast. The photo above taken in the 1880s looks north along Baltimore Street, one of the main routes the fleeing Federals used as they ran, walked, crawled, or otherwise escaped toward the camera's position.

Federal II Corps commander Maj. Gen. Winfield S. Hancock arrived on the field during the afternoon and took command of the Federal forces. His statue (below) sits majestically atop the eastern part of Cemetery Hill, the eminence upon which he and other Federal officers rallied their troops on the evening of July 1.

Thursday, July 2, 1863

During the late afternoon and early evening of July 1, victorious Confederates from Hill's and Ewell's corps chased the broken Federals through town, snatching many more prisoners along the way. General Lee gave Ewell discretion to attack the new Federal position at Cemetery Hill and its ridge to the south, but Ewell elected not to assault it, a decision that is still hotly debated. The first day's fields were strewn with the dead, dying, and grievously wounded of both sides. The Federal I and XI Corps had each lost more than one-third of their number. The two Confederate corps also suffered significant losses. In all, more than 12,000 Federal and Confederate soldiers were counted as casualties by the time the sun set on the first day of July.

Throughout the night, more Federal troops arrived on the battlefield as Meade established a defensive line running from Culp's Hill to the northeast (the right flank) westward to Cemetery Hill, where it curved south and ran for some distance along Cemetery Ridge (the left flank). On the Confederate side, most of General Lee's infantry was on the battlefield by the morning of July 2.

About mid-morning, skirmishing broke out when Federal sharpshooters and cavalry found Confederate infantry moving into the area of Pitzer's Woods. The firefight warned Maj. Gen. Daniel E. Sickles, commander of the Federal III Corps, that Confederates were directly west of his position on the very southern end of the Federal line. Sickles, who did not like the position he was assigned to hold, saw what he thought was higher and better ground to his front along the Emmitsburg Road. Robert E. Lee had already begun formulating plans to attack the Federal flanks, plans that would lead to a very bloody second day at Gettysburg.

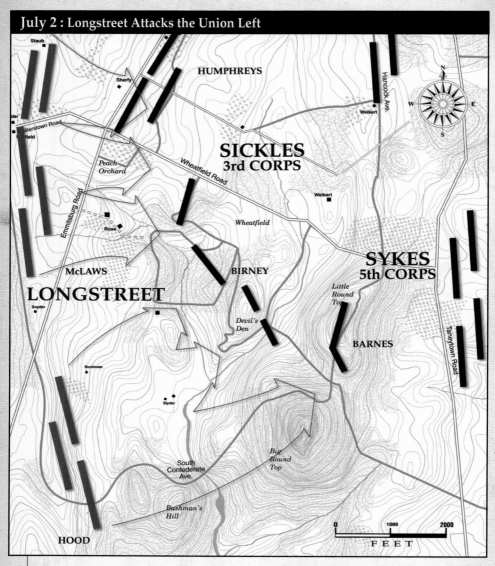

July 2 : Longstreet Attacks the Union Left

(Map labels: Staub, Sherfy, HUMPHREYS, Millerstown Road, field, Peach Orchard, Wheatfield Road, SICKLES 3rd CORPS, Weikert, Hancock Ave., Weikert, Emmitsburg Road, Rose, Wheatfield, McLAWS, BIRNEY, LONGSTREET, Snyder, Devil's Den, SYKES 5th CORPS, Little Round Top, BARNES, Taneytown Road, Bushman, Slyder, South Confederate Ave., Big Round Top, Bushman's Hill, HOOD, FEET, 0 1000 2000)

By mid-afternoon, two divisions (commanded by Maj. Gens. Lafayette McLaws and John B. Hood) of Lt. Gen. James Longstreet's First Corps were marching into position on the southern end of the battlefield to attack the Federal left flank. By that time, however, Sickles had begun marching most of his Union III Corps forward (without orders) toward the higher ground along the Emmitsburg Road. That decision broke off contact with the rest of the Federal line stretching north (see map above) along Cemetery Ridge and put the Federal left flank much closer and farther south than Lee or Longstreet expected it to be.

The photo above was taken from the Confederate position along Seminary Ridge facing southeast and shows a view similar to what General Lee would have had of Little Round Top (left) and Big Round Top (right). Longstreet's 14,000-man assault on the afternoon of July 2 crashed into the Federal flank along the fields and woods from the right toward the Round Tops. The Alfred Waud drawing (below) made a few days after the battle depicts a similar view, with Confederate artillery hammering at Federal infantry and artillery on Little Round Top.

(LIBRARY OF CONGRESS)

65

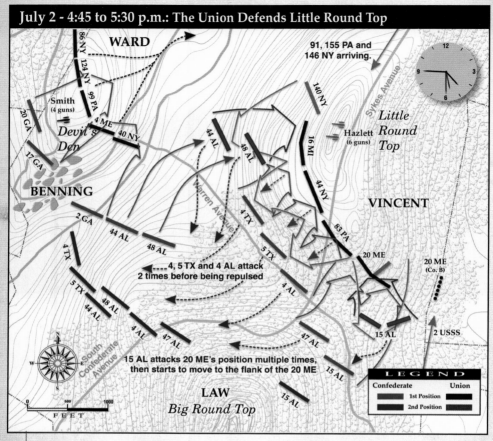

July 2 - 4:45 to 5:30 p.m.: The Union Defends Little Round Top

WARD

91, 155 PA and
146 NY arriving.

86 NY
124 NY
99 PA

140 NY

Little
Round
Top

Smith
(4 guns)

20 GA

Devil's
Den

4 ME
40 NY

44 AL

48 AL

16 NY

Hazlett
(6 guns)

17 GA

44 NY

VINCENT

BENNING

2 GA

4 TX

Warren Avenue

4 TX

5 TX

83 PA

44 AL

48 AL

4, 5 TX and 4 AL attack
2 times before being repulsed

20 ME

20 ME
(Co. B)

5 TX

4 AL

44 AL

48 AL

4 AL

47 AL

47 AL

15 AL

15 AL

2 USSS

South Confederate Avenue

15 AL attacks 20 ME's position multiple times,
then starts to move to the flank of the 20 ME

LEGEND

Confederate   Union

1st Position

2nd Position

0   500   1000
FEET

N
S
W
E

LAW
Big Round Top

15 AL

Sickles' Federal III Corps was unsupported in its new position along the Emmitsburg Road far ahead of the rest of the Federal line. The attack by Longstreet's Confederates against Sickles' exposed position crushed the Federals, sending the survivors reeling back toward the main line along Cemetery Ridge to the east. At the southern end of Longstreet's attacking force, Confederate regiments from Alabama, Texas, and Georgia penetrated east of the Emmitsburg Road and assaulted Federal positions at Devil's Den, Houck's Ridge, and Little Round Top. The extreme southern tip of Little Round Top was defended by Col. Joshua L. Chamberlain's 20th Maine Infantry of Col. Strong Vincent's brigade of the Federal V Corps (see map above). Following repeated assaults by Col. William Oates' 15th Alabama Infantry, the men from Maine fixed their bayonets onto their muskets and charged down the hill into their adversaries - even though Colonel Chamberlain had not yet ordered them to charge. The Federals dispersed the attack and captured many of Oates' soldiers. This ended the Confederate attacks against the end of the Federal left flank.

About 200 yards east of the 20th Maine's left flank (marked with flank marker shown at right) approximately 40 men of Company B were detached as skirmishers during the battle (see map on opposite facing page). Reinforced by 15 men of the 2nd U.S. Sharpshooters, the small group helped their Maine comrades repulse the Alabamians' attacks by firing into the right flank of the attacking Alabama troops.

The Edwin Forbes painting (below) produced about a decade after the battle depicts the Confederate attack against the western face of Little Round Top, which was held by Maj. Gen. George Sykes' V Corps. The romanticized painting shows an attack that never quite materialized. By this time on July 2 it was early evening, and Confederates from Gens. Henry Benning's and Evander Law's brigades were exhausted, disorganized, and had already suffered heavy losses.

67

The stunning photograph above, taken about 1900, depicts one of the most recognizable portrait statues of any battlefield: Brig. Gen. Gouverneur K. Warren. The view looks northwest from Little Round Top. Warren climbed this hill, occupied only by a few signal officers, on the afternoon of July 2 to take in the situation. Sickles had moved most of his corps a half mile to the west, so Warren urged men of the V Corps to mount the hill when he spotted Longstreet's attackers in the distance. Warren's actions saved Little Round Top from falling into enemy hands.

This 1880s photograph (above) taken from the western base of Little Round Top shows Plum Run in the foreground, which flows through what became known as "The Valley of Death." After chasing Federals off the boulders and ridge of Devil's Den in the distance (shown below in a 1909 panorama), Alabamians and Texans swept through the valley to attack Little Round Top. Once the fighting ended, several hundred Confederate and Federal dead and badly wounded were scattered among the rocks and across the valley.

Today, the enormous boulders of Devil's Den are a favorite stop for people who visit the battlefield, especially youngsters who enjoy climbing on the rocks here and throughout the Plum Run Valley. But on the afternoon of July 2, 1863, the entire area (Devil's Den, Houck's Ridge to the north, and the Plum Run Valley to the southeast) was a vast killing ground during Longstreet's assault. When General Sickles marched most of the 10,000-man Federal III Corps forward to the Emmitsburg Road, most of Brig. Gen. Hobart Ward's brigade, about 2,000 soldiers, was posted atop Devil's Den and the high ground of Houck's Ridge, where the brigade formed the extreme left flank of the Army of the Potomac at the time (General Warren had not yet scaled Little Round Top to see that it was undefended). Ward had no support and his men could be easily flanked and routed by any sizeable attacking Confederate force. And, that is exactly what happened when Southerners from Brig. Gen. Jerome Robertson's Brigade attacked Ward during Longstreet's assault (see map below). One-third of Ward's men became casualties by the time his regiments were driven off the rocks and ridge. Capt. James Smith's 4th New York Battery lost four artillery pieces to Robertson's victorious Confederates, who claimed and held Devil's Den for the rest of the battle.

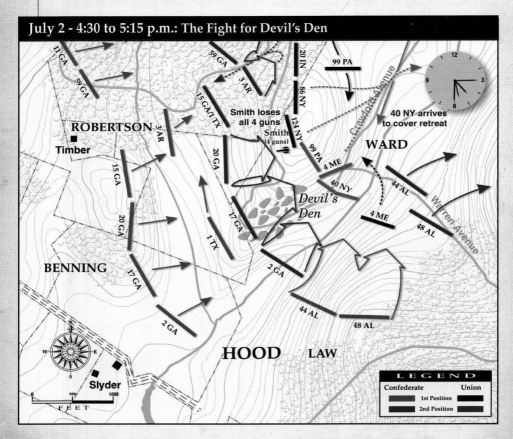

July 2 - 4:30 to 5:15 p.m.: The Fight for Devil's Den

George Rose's farm (above) to the west of Little Round Top sat in nearly the geographic center of Longstreet's assault and therefore became one of the bloodiest farms in American history on July 2. Confederate brigades under Gens. Joseph B. Kershaw and Paul J. Semmes, a total of 3,500 men, attacked from Warfield Ridge eastward toward the Rose Farm (right to left in the photograph) and to Rose's wheatfield farther east. Rose's home still stands, but below are the ruins of his large barn as it appeared in the 1940s. It fell into disrepair, and all that remains of the barn today is the foundation and a few rows of stones.

(NATIONAL PARK SERVICE)

George Rose's wheatfield, known on July 2, 1863 and thereafter as the "Bloody Wheatfield," was the scene of shocking carnage during Longstreet's attack. In sight of Little Round Top, which is just southeast of the field, the large tract of summer wheat changed hands several times as more soldiers of both sides were fed into it. The colorized postcard (above) from the 1880s depicts the northern edge of the Wheatfield with Little Round top in the distance. The 16-foot tall granite monument placed atop a boulder marks the approximate location where Federal Brig. Gen. Samuel K. Zook was mortally wounded leading his II Corps brigade into the Wheatfield.

The three little companies of the 27th Connecticut Infantry, only 75 men all total, have five memorials marking their advance through the Wheatfield. Their regimental monument (left) stands as a testament to the

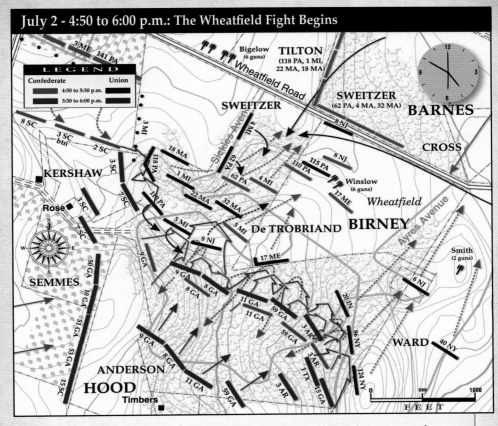

July 2 - 4:50 to 6:00 p.m.: The Wheatfield Fight Begins

37 Connecticut men, half their strength, who fell that day, including their commander Lt. Col. Henry C. Merwin, who was killed near this spot.

As can be seen in the map above, the fighting in Rose's 26-acre patch of wheat late on the afternoon of July 2 was a confusing maelstrom of attacks and counterattacks. Two of Longstreet's divisions under Gens. John B. Hood and Lafayette McLaws, more than 14,000 men, attacked the Federal line from the Joseph Sherfy farm along the Emmitsburg Road at its northern point to the Plum Run Valley at its southernmost point. Sickles' III Corps men were still battling Longstreet's veterans at and around their advanced positions at the Sherfy farm and peach orchard when Rose's wheatfield became the point of attack for portions of three Confederate brigades led by Gens. Joseph B. Kershaw, Paul J. Semmes, and George T. Anderson.

Col. Regis de Trobriand's III Corps brigade, bolstered by a V Corps brigade under Col. Jacob B. Sweitzer and Capt. George B. Winslow's Battery D of the 1st New York Light Artillery, fought valiantly but broke in the face of superior numbers. After this baptism of blood in what would be a prolonged struggle for the wheatfield, nearly a third of the men involved on both sides would fall.

July 2 - 6:20 to 6:50 p.m.: The Union Clears the Wheatfield

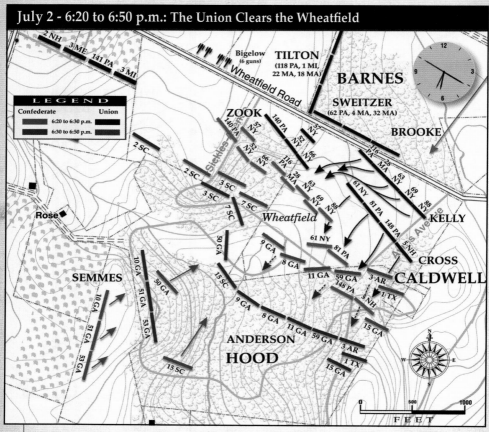

When regiments from the Federal III and V corps were driven out of the field, a II Corps division under Brig. Gen. John C. Caldwell, about 3,300 soldiers, marched south from Cemetery Ridge to reinforce the crumbling left flank of the Union army. The opposing battle lines stretched across the Wheatfield and into the woods north and south of the field. This time the tables turned, a least for a while. After about thirty minutes of vicious fighting, three of Caldwell's brigades under Brig. Gen. Samuel K. Zook and Cols. Edward E. Cross and Patrick Kelly cleared the Wheatfield and held the Confederates to its southern edge. The fighting came at a heavy price in killed and wounded including two brigade commanders. Zook, as noted above, was mortally wounded. Earlier that same day Colonel Cross predicted his own death when he informed his corps commander, Maj. Gen. Winfield S. Hancock, that the fight would be his last. Cross was overseeing his men on his left flank in the woods south of the Wheatfield when he was mortally struck by a Confederate bullet. Nearly 40% of the men in his brigade were killed, wounded, or captured before their evening in the hellish Wheatfield ended.

One of the most popular and iconic monuments on the Gettysburg battlefield is dedicated to three of the five regiments of Col. Patrick Kelly's II Corps "Irish Brigade" (right). Dedicated in 1888, inscribed on its Celtic cross of polished granite are the three regiments – the 63rd, 69th, and 88th New York Infantry. Battlefield visitors find it hard to resist a close examination of the bronze sculpture of the Irish wolf hound on the base, which represents faith and devotion in its reclined pose. Many also find it hard to resist the tradition of placing dog biscuits between the loyal animal's paws.

Shrouded in fog, the lonely monument for Capt. George B. Winslow's battery (1st New York Light Artillery) rests on a high point just north of the center of the Wheatfield. Dedicated in 1888, the monument celebrates the selfless support Winslow and his gunners provided for Federal infantry early in the fighting against attacking Georgians and South Carolinians.

The summer sun was dropping behind South Mountain on July 2 when a final Confederate push through Rose's field of trampled corpse-strewn wheat began. A Federal II Corps brigade commanded by Col. John R. Brooke made the deepest incursion against the Southerners and held back part of Semmes' Brigade at the base of a slight ridge south of George Rose's house. Surrounded by overwhelming numbers of Confederates, though, Brooke had to give up his ground.

The Federals fighting in the Wheatfield, eventually reinforced by Regular Army regiments under Cols. Hannibal Day and Sidney Burbank, were swept out of the area when four Confederate regiments attacked from two directions. That night it may well have been possible to walk or jump from one corpse or wounded man to the next all the way across the Wheatfield in any direction without ever having to touch the ground. Many of the badly wounded suvivors of both sides had to lie in the wheatfield all that night and throughout the next day before they could receive any care or comfort.

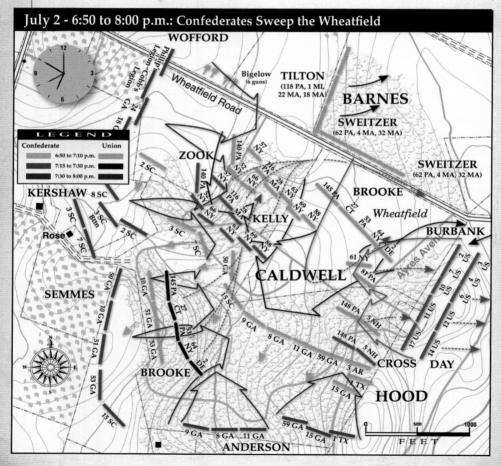

July 2 - 6:50 to 8:00 p.m.: Confederates Sweep the Wheatfield

(LIBRARY OF CONGRESS)

This photograph (above), taken in the 1880s by Gettysburg photographer William H. Tipton, shows Joseph Sherfy's Peach Orchard along the Emmitsburg Road. Federal III Corps commander Maj. Gen. Daniel E. Sickles made the spot the most famous grove of peach trees in the world when he advanced most of his corps forward to his new position just before 4:00 p.m. on July 2. Longstreet's attack swirled over Sherfy's property, including his house and his large barn (below).

July 2 - 5:30 to 7:20 p.m.: The Peach Orchard and Trostle Farm

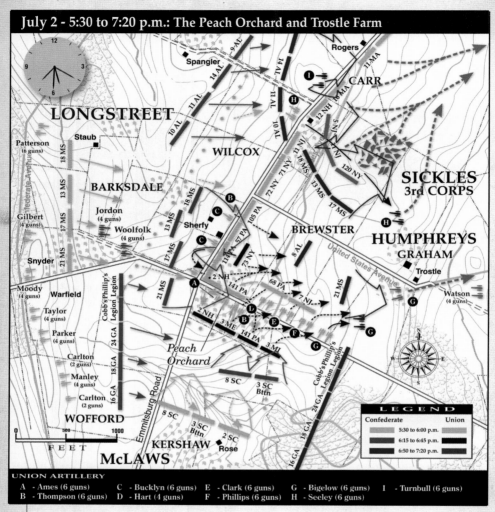

UNION ARTILLERY

A - Ames (6 guns)   C - Bucklyn (6 guns)   E - Clark (6 guns)   G - Bigelow (6 guns)   I - Turnbull (6 guns)
B - Thompson (6 guns)   D - Hart (4 guns)   F - Phillips (6 guns)   H - Seeley (6 guns)

When Sickles' advanced line along Sherfy's Peach Orchard and the Emmitsburg Road broke under the weight of Longstreet's assault early that evening (which was directly supported by a brigade of Alabama troops on his immediate left under Brig. Gen. Cadmus M. Wilcox of Lt. Gen. A. P. Hill's Third Corps), the routed Federals fled east and north toward the main Union line along Cemetery Ridge (see map above). The Southerners controlled the high ground at the Peach Orchard for the rest of the battle.

By the time the fighting ended here on July 2, Sickles' 10,000 men had suffered nearly 40% casualties including Sickles himself, whose leg was nearly blown off by a Confederate shell. The general eventually lost his leg but survived, though he never led troops in the field again.

Federal artillery played a key role in the fighting here on July 2. Numerous batteries were posted in support of the Union soldiers along the Wheatfield Road (an unnamed road in 1863 connecting the Emmitsburg Road with the Taneytown Road to the south), and the Emmitsburg Road. Working to cover the withdrawal of the embattled infantry, many of these gunners were among the last to leave. The 9th Battery of the Massachusetts Light Artillery commanded by Capt. John Bigelow suffered heavy losses conducting a fighting withdrawal toward and beyond the Abraham Trostle farm, seen above in a photo taken a few days after the battle. Bigelow lost many men and nearly all his battery's horses, which were still visible on the devastated Trostle farm.

To the right is the monument for the 73rd New York Infantry, one of Sickles' regiments and comprised mostly of former New York City firemen. They dedicated this sculpture in 1897 to commemorate their stand on July 2—and their dual identity. The fireman holds a calling horn, symbolically beckoning the men to their solemn duty.

Cavalry was also involved in fighting on July 2. The village of Hunterstown, four miles northeast of Gettysburg, was near the Confederate left flank during the battle. When Maj. Gen. J.E.B. Stuart arrived at Gettysburg that afternoon after his long ride through Maryland and Pennsylvania with three brigades of his cavalry, Brig. Gen. Wade Hampton's brigade rode through Hunterstown. The Federal 3rd Cavalry Division under Brig. Gen. H. Judson Kilpatrick approached Hunterstown behind Hampton and clashed with the Confederates' rearguard at the Hunterstown village square, shown here in an early 1900s photograph taken by Gettysburg photographer William H. Tipton. The small Confederate detail and the pursuing Federals galloped toward the camera's position.

Already on the road to Gettysburg, Hampton turned his forces around to face northeast to counter the threat posed by the Union cavalry. One of Kilpatrick's brigade commanders, George A. Custer, had been promoted to brigadier general only a few days earlier. When Custer saw Hampton's rearguard standing defiantly in the road leading to Gettysburg, he personally led a single company of his 6th Michigan Cavalry in a mounted charge down the road – Custer's first mounted charge as a brigadier general during the Civil War. In 2009, a local historical group dedicated a monument (left) to Custer's Hunterstown fight, the only

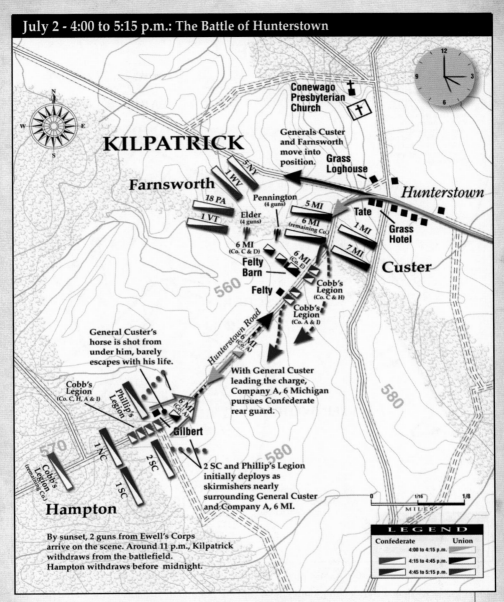

July 2 - 4:00 to 5:15 p.m.: The Battle of Hunterstown

KILPATRICK

Farnsworth

Conewago
Presbyterian
Church

Generals Custer
and Farnsworth
move into
position.

Grass
Loghouse

Hunterstown

5 NY
1 WV
18 PA
1 VT

Pennington
(4 guns)

Elder
(4 guns)

5 MI

6 MI
(remaining Co.)

Tate

1 MI

7 MI

Grass
Hotel

Custer

6 MI
(Co. C & D)

6 MI
(Co. E)

Felty
Barn

Felty

Cobb's
Legion
(Co. C & H)

Cobb's
Legion
(Co. A & D)

560

General Custer's
horse is shot from
under him, barely
escapes with his life.

With General Custer
leading the charge,
Company A, 6 Michigan
pursues Confederate
rear guard.

Cobb's
Legion
(Co. C, H, A & I)

Phillip's
Legion

6 MI
(Co. A)

Gilbert

580

2 SC and Phillip's Legion
initially deploys as
skirmishers nearly
surrounding General Custer
and Company A, 6 MI.

570

1 NC

2 SC

580

Cobb's
Legion
(remaining Co.)

1 SC

Hampton

By sunset, 2 guns from Ewell's Corps
arrive on the scene. Around 11 p.m., Kilpatrick
withdraws from the battlefield.
Hampton withdraws before midnight.

0   1/16   1/8
MILES

LEGEND
Confederate   Union
4:00 to 4:15 p.m.
4:15 to 4:45 p.m.
4:45 to 5:15 p.m.

monument on the Hunterstown battlefield.

Custer nearly lost his life at Hunterstown. During the charge, his horse was shot and he was pinned underneath (see map above). A Michigan private shot a Rebel who was about to saber Custer and rescued him. After a Confederate countercharge was repulsed, an artillery duel lasted until nightfall. The Confederate left flank was secure when Kilpatrick withdrew under cover of darkness.

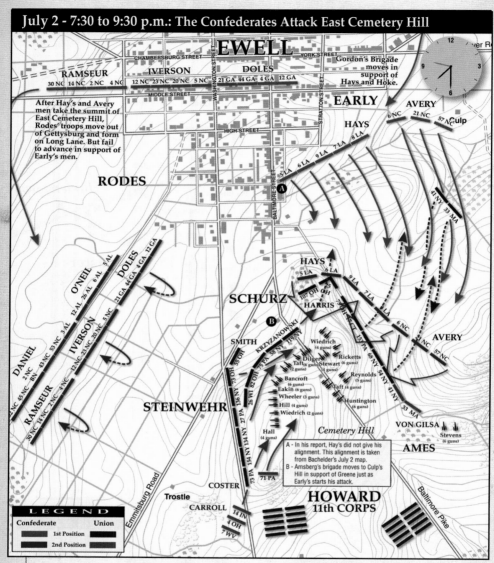

July 2 - 7:30 to 9:30 p.m.: The Confederates Attack East Cemetery Hill

A - In his report, Hay's did not give his alignment. This alignment is taken from Bachelder's July 2 map.
B - Amsberg's brigade moves to Culp's Hill in support of Greene just as Early's starts his attack.

LEGEND
Confederate   Union
        1st Position
        2nd Position

The commander of the Confederate Second Corps, Lt. Gen. Richard S. Ewell, decided against attacking the Federal rallying point atop Cemetery Hill on the first day of the battle. Part of Gen. Lee's plan for July 2 was for Ewell to attack the northeast side of the hill once Longstreet's assault against the Federal left flank was underway. It was after 7:00 p.m. before Ewell was ready to attack, and by that time Cemetery Hill had been fortified with troops of the XI Corps and ringed with nearly two dozen cannon (see map above).

Night was falling when part of Maj. Gen. Jubal A. Early's Division attacked

East Cemetery Hill from the north and east. Brig. Gen. Harry Hays' Louisiana brigade plus North Carolinians pierced the Union defenses and fought a vicious hand-to-hand combat that won part of the hill. Unfortunately for the South, reinforcements from Maj. Gen. Robert E. Rodes got into position too late and fell back without entering the fight. The Confederate assault was beaten back when more XI troops reinforced the defenders. The hill remained in Federal hands. Already badly bloodied on July 1, the XI Corps suffered more casualties that brought the total to more than 40% of its strength. Hays lost 25% of his hard-fighting Louisianans in the attack.

The 1878 photograph at right shows a wooden observation tower that stood on East Cemetery Hill but was later removed. The Evergreen Cemetery Gatehouse (below), an iconic fixture of the battlefield, still stands today atop Cemetery Hill as a mute witness of the Gettysburg carnage.

The fighting that took place at the anchor of the Federal right flank on Culp's Hill is overshadowed today by the lore surrounding combat at other Gettysburg landmarks like Little Round Top, Devil's Den, and the Bloody Wheatfield. Few people realize that longer sustained fighting took place on Culp's Hill than at any other location on the battlefield. Beginning on July 2, the Federal defensive line stretched for more than two miles (the Confederate line was more than twice that distance) from Little Round Top in the south to Culp's Hill to the north. The attack against Culp's Hill got underway while the Confederates were attacking East Cemetery Hill in the gathering darkness to the northwest. Maj. Gen. Edward "Allegheny" Johnson's Division of Ewell's Second Corps crossed Rock Creek and attacked the XII Corps Federal brigade on the summit commanded by Brig. Gen. George S. Greene.

When Greene's New Yorkers were in danger of being flanked on their right to the south, timely reinforcements in the form of I and XI Corps regiments rushed to Greene's aid. Johnson's men assaulted Culp's Hill at least four times, but the tenacious Federals held on. The fight for Culp's Hill had lasted well into the night, and although some lodgments were made, the hill remained in Federal hands.

Visitors to Culp's Hill today will notice that the hill in 1863, as portrayed in Edwin

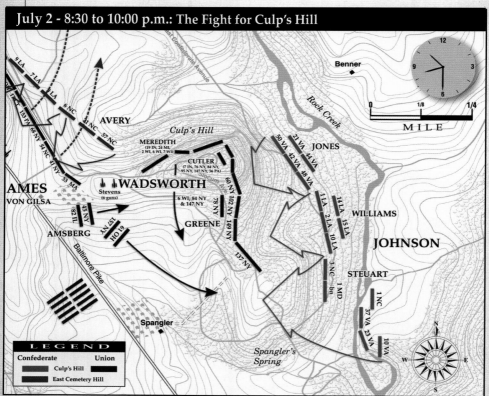

July 2 - 8:30 to 10:00 p.m.: The Fight for Culp's Hill

(LIBRARY OF CONGRESS)

Forbes' painting above, was much less wooded. The view in the painting looks west from the area of Rock Creek toward the Federal position atop the hill, with General Johnson's Confederates attacking in the foreground.

A favorite area of the battlefield for children and adults alike is Spangler's Spring, which rests in a saddle south of Culp's Hill between that eminence and a smaller hill called "Lower Culp's Hill." As it is today for tourists, the spring was a popular picnic area among locals prior to the battle. On July 2 and 3, 1863, though, the area was hotly contested by the armies. XII Corps Federals controlled the ground on July 2 until the area was lost to Confederates of Brig. Gen. George H. Steuart's Brigade of Johnson's Division during the attack that evening. The following day the Federals regained the ground. The photograph at right, taken in 1903, shows the popular spring with the present concrete enclosure built by the War Department in 1895. The spring dried up sometime later, and although it was fed by a water pipe for some years afterward, no water flows to the spring today.

(LIBRARY OF CONGRESS)

85

By the end of July 2, Maj. Gen. George G. Meade's Army of the Potomac had lost nearly one in five (20%) of his 95,000-man army. Robert E. Lee's Army of Northern Virginia's losses were also heavy at roughly the same ratio for his smaller 75,000-man army. From the moment the first casualty fell on the morning of July 1, both armies had to deal with their dead and care for the dying and wounded. Much of this responsibility fell upon the citizens of the town and surrounding areas.

Nearly every building in and around the town was turned into a makeshift hospital, including the barn on the Daniel Lady farm (above), which housed many of the Confederates wounded during the July 2 fight for Culp's Hill. Because medical equipment and medicines were in short supply, as were medical personnel, overburdened civilians had to make do with what they had on hand. Mostly they tried to make the wounded as comfortable as possible. There was little else they could do.

Robert E. Lee's July 2 hammering assaults against both Federal flanks came close several times to breaking through and capturing key terrain, but despite the valiant efforts of his veteran troops the attacks failed to dislodge the equally valiant Union defenders. Lee knew how close he had come and was determined to remain on the offensive on July 3. He believed that one more concerted effort by his men would crack Meade's line open and force him to retreat.

The only question was where he would attack.

Friday, July 3, 1863

Both armies spent the evening of July 2 tending to their wounded and processing prisoners while the rank and file – privates, corporals, and sergeants – counted noses in their companies and regiments to determine their unit strength. Ammunition was replenished, food (if it was to be had) was eaten, and many penned lines in diaries recounting the horrors of the day. Along the Federal line at such places as Cemetery Hill, Cemetery Ridge, and Little Round Top, artillery crews repaired and readied their guns, just as their Confederate counterparts did along Seminary Ridge, Warfield Ridge, and on Benner's Hill northeast of Culp's Hill.

J.E.B. Stuart's Confederate cavalry had finally arrived late the previous day and now secured the left flank of the Army of Northern Virginia, where the troopers tried to snatch a little rest after their grueling 200-mile journey into Pennsylvania. Opposite Stuart was Brig. Gen. David Gregg's Federal cavalry division, which anchored the Army of the Potomac's right flank near the Hanover Road. Both armies closely guarded their respective supply wagons in rear of their lines, and skirmishers played their deadly game well ahead of the main lines of battle. Nearly everyone expected more bloody combat on the morrow.

That evening about midnight General Meade held a council of war with his top officers, who encouraged Meade to remain in his present position and fight it out the next day. When the meeting broke up, Meade took aside Brig. Gen. John Gibbon. Gibbon commanded a division in General Hancock's II Corps, which was holding the center of the army's line along Cemetery Ridge. "If Lee attacks to-morrow," Meade told Gibbon, "it will be on your front."

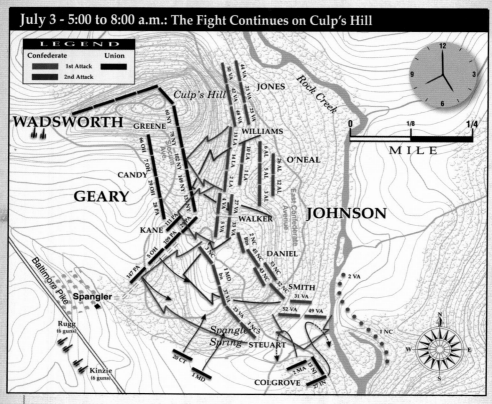

July 3 - 5:00 to 8:00 a.m.: The Fight Continues on Culp's Hill

Throughout the night of July 2 and into the early morning hours of July 3, additional Federal troops marched to the right flank to reinforce Culp's Hill. The rest of Maj. Gen. Henry W. Slocum's XII Corps returned there from the southern part of the field (where it was only lightly engaged on July 2). Those additional troops would be needed by Brig. Gen. John W. Geary, the division leader in command of the brigades defending the hill, because Confederate reinforcements also arrived in preparation for a renewed attack on July 3.

About an hour before dawn, the Federals launched a spoiling attack that opened with a short but powerful artillery barrage followed by localized infantry attacks that captured ground lost the day before. The fighting had begun in earnest long before the Confederates had planned or hoped. On Lower Culp's Hill farther south near Spangler's Spring, Federals of the 1st Maryland Potomac Home Guard attacked the Confederates but could not dislodge them (see map above). The Marylanders withdrew and marched to the top of the hill. The 20th Connecticut of Col. Archibald L. McDougall's brigade advanced and began a five-hour firefight with Southerners from Brig. Gen. George H. Steuart's Brigade.

By the time the sun broke over the horizon behind the Rebel lines east of the hill,

the Federal XII Corps and its supports were in a full-scale fight with six veteran Confederate brigades.

The Confederates attempted several unsuccessful assaults against the Federal breastworks ringing Culp's Hill, as portrayed by Edwin Forbes in his famous painting above. General Steuart prepared his men for one final assault south of the hill (depicted in the *Battles and Leaders* drawing below), but as they advanced through an open field, musket fire from Brig. Gen. Thomas L. Kane's Ohioans and Pennsylvanians brought them to a halt.

By noon, the seven-hour slugfest for Culp's Hill was over. The vital Federal supply line running along the Baltimore Pike between the hill and the rest of the Federal line farther south was secure.

One of Brig. Gen. John Buford's Federal cavalry brigades was still south of Gettysburg near Emmitsburg, Maryland, on the morning of July 3. Its commander, Brig. Gen. Wesley Merritt, received orders to ride to the battlefield, but as he prepared to do so a civilian approached and told Merritt that several Confederate wagons behind Robert E. Lee's lines were lightly guarded and could be easily captured near his farm at Fairfield, about eight miles southwest of Gettysburg. Merritt sent the 6th U.S. Cavalry to Fairfield to secure the wagons while he rode with his remaining regiments to Gettysburg.

Maj. Samuel H. Starr, in command of the 6th U.S. Cavalry, reached Fairfield in the early afternoon. The Confederate wagons, loaded with plunder from Pennsylvania, were actually well guarded, and Starr's 400 troopers battled with three regiments

(KEVIN BREAM)

July 3 - 1:00 to 1:45 p.m.: The Battle of Fairfield

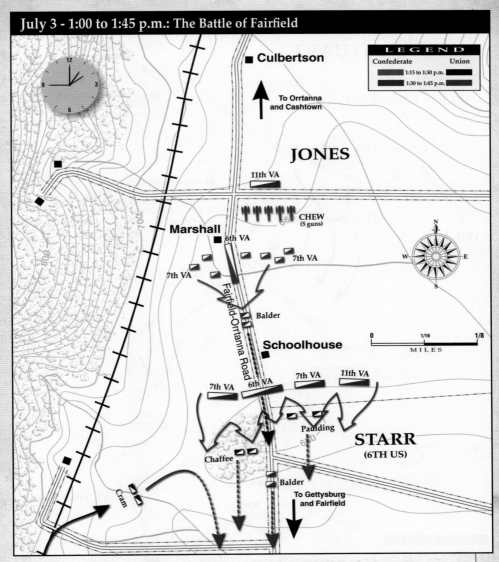

of Virginia cavalry led by Brig. Gen. William E. Jones posted at the Benjamin Marshall home (top of opposite facing page). Several men from Starr's heavily outnumbered command were killed and wounded, and more than one-half of the regiment was captured. (See map above).

Merritt squandered an opportunity to block Lee's line of retreat through Fairfield and the mountain passes to the south by sending such a small force against an enemy of unknown strength. The surviving 6th U.S. Cavalry veterans held their postwar reunions at the Marshall home and placed a placard there to memorialize the day their regiment was nearly wiped out not far from Gettysburg. (Bottom of opposite facing page.)

July 3 - 1:00 to 2:00 p.m.: The Fight at East Cavalry Field

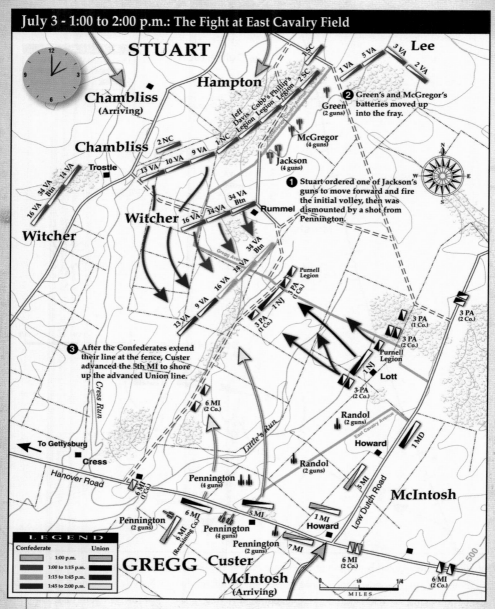

After watching part of the Stonewall Brigade (Ewell's Confederate corps) engage
David Gregg's cavalry division at Brinkerhoff's Ridge on the evening of July 2, J.E.B.
Stuart moved most of his cavalry out of its camps early on the morning of July 3. If
Gregg's cavalry was still there, Stuart intended to flush them out.

Gregg and his cavalry were indeed still on the Federal right flank. Stuart fired
one of his cannons to Stuart fired one of his cannons to get a response from Gregg,

and sent dismounted skirmishers from his position along Cress Ridge toward the John Rummel farm and Gregg's position. Brig. Gen. George A. Custer's brigade of Michigan cavalry was in the area but belonged to another division. When Gregg asked Custer to stay and fight to counter Stuart's threat, Custer agreed.

Artillery rounds were flying above Rummel's fields when Stuart's and Gregg's skirmish lines met along a lane running from the Hanover Road to Rummel's farm buildings. The William H. Tipton photograph below was taken after the battle and shows the damaged Rummel barn in the center (which still stands today), which suffered shell and bullet damage. The lane leading north to the buildings is visible in the foreground.

In 1889, Custer's Michigan cavalry regiments dedicated their massive monument (above right) on the field south of Rummel's buildings. It was here the Michiganders met the Rebel cavalry in a final mounted charge that repulsed Stuart's threat against the right and rear of the Federal position at Gettysburg.

(NATIONAL PARK SERVICE)

July 3 - 2:15 to 3:00 p.m.: The Fight at East Cavalry Field

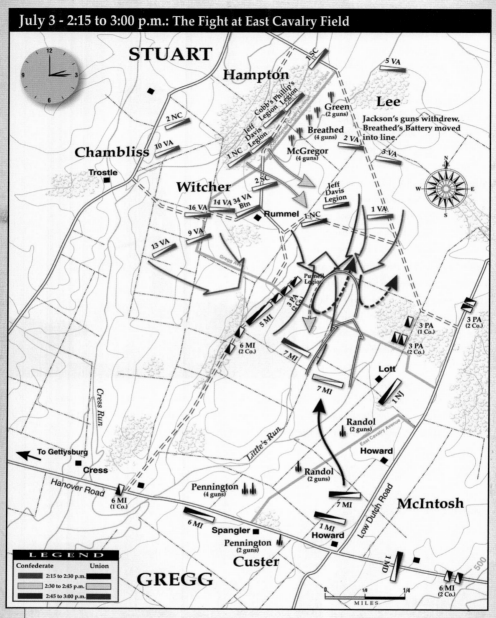

In the first series of mounted combat, Custer's 7th Michigan countercharged into the face of mounted assaults by elements of Brig. Gens. Fitzhugh Lee's and Wade Hampton's brigades (see map above). The Confederates were held to a fence line southeast of the Rummel farm buildings. One final mounted charge awaited the blue and gray horsemen.

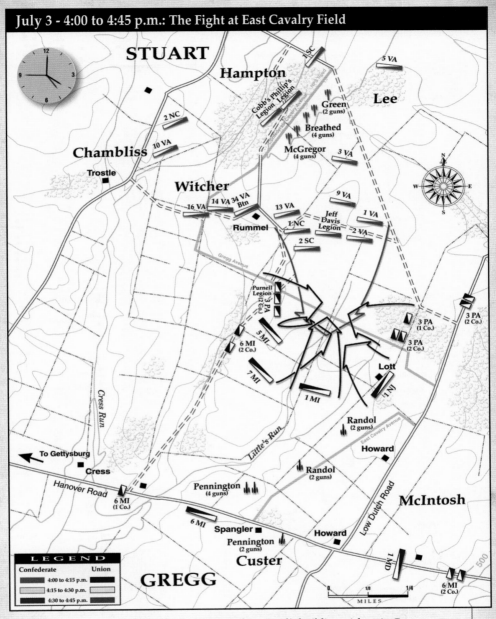

July 3 - 4:00 to 4:45 p.m.: The Fight at East Cavalry Field

Stuart sent in one final heavy assault east of Rummel's buildings (above). Custer formed up the men of his 1st Michigan Cavalry, then spurred his horse and led them in a countercharge, shouting "Come on, you Wolverines!" Men, horses, and steel collided like two massive waves crashing against one another. Hit from three sides by Custer's and Gregg's troopers, Stuart's attack was thrown back.

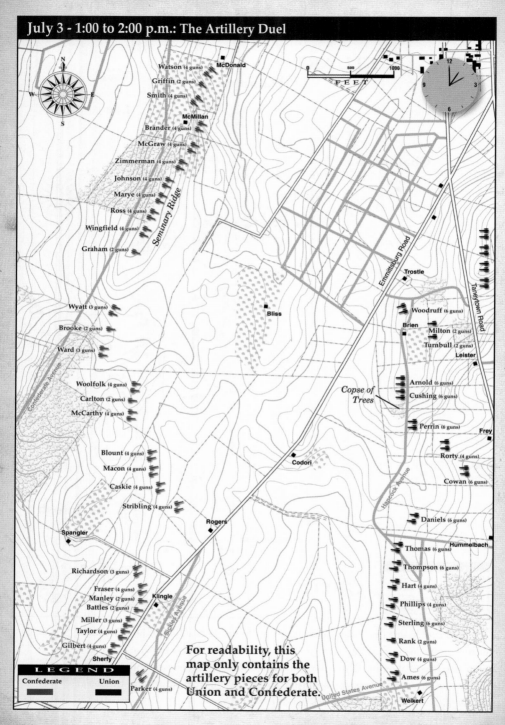

July 3 - 1:00 to 2:00 p.m.: The Artillery Duel

Watson (4 guns)
McDonald
Griffin (2 guns)
Smith (4 guns)
McMillan
Brander (4 guns)
McGraw (4 guns)
Zimmerman (4 guns)
Johnson (4 guns)
Marye (4 guns)
Ross (4 guns)
Wingfield (4 guns)
Graham (2 guns)

Seminary Ridge

Wyatt (3 guns)
Brooke (2 guns)
Ward (3 guns)

Woolfolk (4 guns)
Carlton (2 guns)
McCarthy (4 guns)

Blount (4 guns)
Macon (4 guns)
Caskie (4 guns)
Stribling (4 guns)

Spangler
Rogers

Richardson (3 guns)
Fraser (4 guns)
Manley (2 guns)
Klingle
Battles (2 guns)
Miller (3 guns)
Taylor (4 guns)
Gilbert (4 guns)
Sherfy
Parker (4 guns)

Bliss

Trostle
Woodruff (6 guns)
Brien
Milton (2 guns)
Turnbull (2 guns)
Leister

Arnold (6 guns)
Cushing (6 guns)

Copse of Trees

Codori

Perrin (6 guns)
Frey

Rorty (4 guns)

Cowan (6 guns)

Daniels (6 guns)
Hummelbach

Thomas (6 guns)
Thompson (6 guns)
Hart (4 guns)
Phillips (4 guns)
Sterling (6 guns)
Rank (2 guns)
Dow (4 guns)
Ames (6 guns)

Weikert

Emmittsburg Road
Taneytown Road
Hancock Avenue
Confederate Avenue
Sickles Avenue
United States Avenue

For readability, this map only contains the artillery pieces for both Union and Confederate.

FEET
0   500   1000

LEGEND
Confederate   Union

J.E.B. Stuart's independent cavalry thrust at Rummel's farm was underway four miles east of Gettysburg about the same time the large-scale artillery bombardment preceding Lee's infantry assault against the center of the Union line along Cemetery Ridge opened fire. At or near 1:00 p.m. on July 3, as many as 150 Confederate cannon arrayed opposite the Union line opened fire. The Federals had some 115 guns aimed at Lee's line along Seminary Ridge. (See map on opposite facing page, which shows only the artillery placements for clarity.)

After attacking Meade's flanks on July 2 failed, Lee decided to send a column numbering about 13,000 infantry against roughly the center of the Federal line just south of the town's cemetery. In order to soften the resistance and perhaps drive the defenders away along the stone wall atop the ridge, he pounded it with artillery. When Lee's cannon opened early that afternoon by launching their missiles of death at Cemetery Ridge, the Federal cannons responded, as shown in a detail from the 1883 Cyclorama painting below.

(NATIONAL PARK SERVICE)

July 3 - 2:00 to 2:45 p.m.: Pickett's Charge

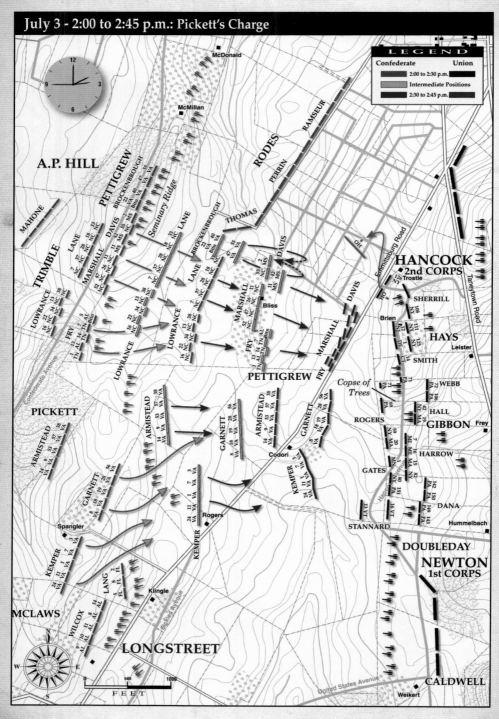

LEGEND

Confederate   Union

2:00 to 2:30 p.m.

Intermediate Positions

2:30 to 2:45 p.m.

McDonald

McMillan

A.P. HILL

PETTIGREW

Seminary Ridge

BROCKENBROUGH

MAHONE

TRIMBLE

LANE

DAVIS

MARSHALL

LOWRANCE

FRY

Confederate Avenue

BROCKENBROUGH

LANE

THOMAS

RODES

PERRIN

RAMSEUR

DAVIS

Old

Emmitsburg Road

Taneytown Road

HANCOCK
2nd CORPS

Trostle

SHERRILL

Brien

HAYS

Leister

SMITH

MARSHALL

Bliss

FRY

PETTIGREW

MARSHALL

FRY

PICKETT

ARMISTEAD

GARNETT

ARMISTEAD

GARNETT

Codori

KEMPER

Copse of Trees

ROGERS

WEBB

HALL

GIBBON

Frey

HARROW

GATES

DANA

Hummelbach

DOUBLEDAY

NEWTON
1st CORPS

STANNARD

Spangler

GARNETT

Rogers

KEMPER

LANG

Klingle

Sickles Avenue

MCLAWS

WILCOX

LONGSTREET

Hancock Avenue

Weikert

United States Avenue

CALDWELL

FEET
0   500   1000

The cannonade lasted about one hour and was the largest and longest artillery duel in American history. The cannon fire was subsiding when three divisions of infantry – composed of soldiers from Virginia, Alabama, Tennessee, and North Carolina – stepped into formation along Seminary Ridge. Although the assault has become known as "Pickett's Charge," Maj. Gen. George Pickett led only one of the divisions involved. The other two were under the command of Maj. Gen. Isaac Trimble and Brig. Gen. J. Johnston Pettigrew. The Edwin Forbes painting above captures the Confederate perspective looking toward the Federal line.

At right is the Virginia Memorial dedicated in 1917 at what is popularly known as the "Point of Woods" along Seminary Ridge. Robert E. Lee watched the progress of "Pickett's Charge" from this area for a time, and met many of the retreating survivors here.

The 13,000 Confederates began their long and deadly mile-long walk toward Cemetery Ridge as drummer boys pounded out a march beat. Union artillerists hurled solid and exploding shells at advancing infantry, cutting down hundreds of Southerners before they made it even halfway across the open fields. The survivors closed ranks and continued onward.

The 1909 panorama below was taken from the Ziegler's Grove observation tower (which has since been removed). Pickett's Charge rolled toward the Federal line from right to left along the postwar park road (Hancock Avenue) in the center-right. The Round Tops are visible in the center distance at the southern tip (left flank) of the Federal line. On the far left is the little white farm house of Lydia Leister, which served as George Meade's headquarters during the battle. The park road in the picture, removed in the 1900s, connected the Leister property with Hancock Avenue.

Federals from both the I Corps (now under Maj. Gen. John Newton) and the II Corps under Maj. Gen. Winfield Scott Hancock, including men in the 72nd Pennsylvania Infantry (whose monument is shown above left) waited anxiously along the stone wall for the oncoming enemy to reach them.

Along the stone wall at roughly the center of the area hit by Pickett's Charge was a small clump of trees. After the war, a Virginia veteran from Pickett's Division told Gettysburg historian John B. Bachelder the clump, or "copse" of trees, was the focal point of the charge. Thereafter, the copse became symbolic of the pinnacle of the assault, and the "High Water Mark" memorial, which features a bronze book listing all the commands participating in the charge (above), was dedicated there in 1892.

General Hancock rode on his horse up and down his line and encouraged his men to remain in place and be ready to receive the Confederate assault. Once most of the Southerners crossed the Emmitsburg Road a few hundred yards away from the main Federal line, the 13th and 16th Vermont Infantry regiments at the southern end of Hancock's line marched forward a short distance and swung to the right, placing themselves on the flank of the Confederate line. (See map on opposite facing page.) Hancock was watching the Vermonters pour devastating musket volleys into Brig. Gen. James L. Kemper's Virginians when he was shot in the inside of his thigh. He was helped off his horse and a tourniquet applied so he could remain to oversee the fighting and witness the repulse of the massive attack. In 1888, a small stone marker (above) was placed to mark the area where Hancock fell wounded.

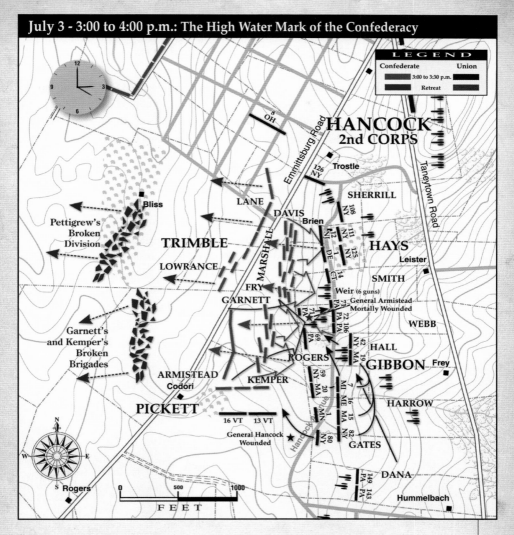

July 3 - 3:00 to 4:00 p.m.: The High Water Mark of the Confederacy

LEGEND

Confederate Union

3:00 to 3:30 p.m.

Retreat

8 OH

HANCOCK
2nd CORPS

126 NY Trostle

Bliss

SHERRILL

LANE

108 NY

Pettigrew's
Broken
Division

DAVIS
Brien

112 NY

111 NY

TRIMBLE

1 DE

125 NY

HAYS

LOWRANCE

14 CT

Leister

SMITH

FRY

Weir (6 guns)

71 PA

72 PA

General Armistead
Mortally Wounded

GARNETT

106 PA

WEBB

69 PA

Garnett's
and Kemper's
Broken
Brigades

42 NY

19 MA

HALL

ROGERS

GIBBON Frey

ARMISTEAD
Codori

KEMPER

59 NY

20 MA

7 MI

HARROW

PICKETT

16 ME

15 MA

82 NY

16 VT   13 VT

1 MN

80 NY

GATES

General Hancock
Wounded

N

W   E

S   Rogers

149 PA

143 PA

DANA

0   500   1000

FEET

Hummelbach

Because of the heavy Federal artillery and musket fire, only perhaps one-third
(4,000 or 5,000) of the Confederates who had stepped off Seminary Ridge advanced
beyond the Emmitsburg Road. From the Abram Brian farm to the north (his barn is
shown at bottom of the opposite facing page, with the 111th New York Infantry monument) and south along the stone wall, sheets of flame cut down the advancing gray infantry. Many of the Confederate survivors who made it all the way to the Federal line
engaged in hand-to-hand combat in a final desperate struggle to break the defenses.

Just to the north of the Copse of Trees, one of Pickett's brigade commanders,
Brig. Gen. Lewis A. Armistead, led perhaps a few dozen of his Virginians over the
stone wall. Armistead held his hat aloft on the tip of his sword so his men could see
him. With a cry of "Give them the cold steel!" Armistead and his small group pushed

aside some of the soldiers from the Federal Philadelphia Brigade under Brig. Gen. Alexander Webb and fell upon Lt. Alonzo Cushing's Federal artillery battery. Already wounded, the 22-year-old Cushing remained with his guns to fire another round and was killed when a bullet struck him in his open mouth.

Armistead placed a hand on one of the guns and urged his men forward but was shot down and his men surrounded. One of Hancock's staff officers came to Armistead's aide. When the general was informed that his old army friend Hancock had also been badly wounded, Armistead is said to have expressed his regret that both of them had been wounded while battling against one another.

Fully one-half of Armistead's men were killed, wounded, or captured. Southern losses were staggering across the board. Fewer than one-half of the 13,000 men from the three Confederate divisions who stepped off Seminary Ridge made it back safely after the assault. Some Southern regiments lost as many as eight out of every 10 men. The 14th Tennessee Infantry of A. P. Hill's Corps suffered catastrophic losses. The small regiment had already lost more than 300 of its 365 men on the first day of the battle. It went into Pickett's Charge with about 60 men and emerged with just three.

General Lee met some of the survivors, many of them also wounded, as they made their way back to the Confederate line. He accepted the blame for the failure of the grand assault and told them so. To General Pickett, Lee stated, "Your men did all men could do," and advised his division leaded to prepare for a possible counterassault.

Pickett responded, "General Lee, I have no division now."

Along the Federal line atop Cemetery Ridge, Union soldiers corralled their Confederate prisoners and tended to the wounded of both sides. The nearly one mile of ground between the two lines was a shocking scene of indescribable carnage. The Federals took stock of what they had just accomplished - the repulse of one of the largest massed infantry assaults of the war. A few of the Federals began to cheer. What began inside a handful of throats spread through the ranks like a wave, rippling through Hancock's men as it rolled south to their comrades who had also been badly bloodied the day before during Longstreet's July 2 assault. The verbal celebration even spread to the Federals perched atop Little Round Top as thousands upon thousands of General Meade's men cheered their throats hoarse. After suffering defeat after humiliating defeat at the hands of Lee's vaunted army, they finally realized what they had done. Rebel survivors, meanwhile, continued making their way back to their lines. Their journey could only have been that much harder having to listen to the sound of defeat washing over them in an entirely new form.

The detail from the Cyclorama painting below depicts the climax of the struggle at the stone wall, with the Copse of Trees near the center. Note the Round Tops in the distance and the puffs of smoke atop Little Round Top, from which Federal batteries fired into the charging Confederates from more than one mile away.

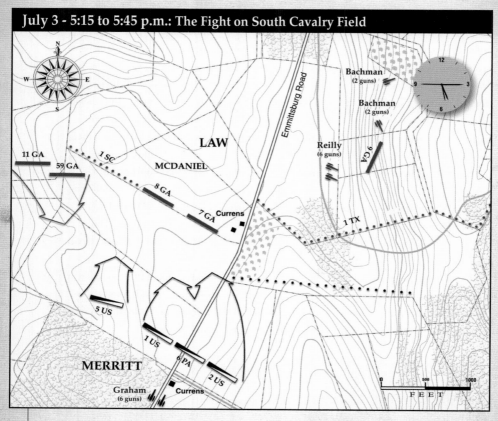

July 3 - 5:15 to 5:45 p.m.: The Fight on South Cavalry Field

The repulse of Pickett's Charge at the center of the battlefield was not the end of the fighting on July 3. Slightly more than a mile to the south, along the Emmitsburg Road and east toward Big Round Top, Federal cavalry units assaulted the Confederate right flank just as Pickett's Charge was being turned back. Four regiments of Regular U.S. Cavalry under Brig. Gen. Wesley Merritt reached the battlefield on July 3 from Emmitsburg, Maryland. Merritt's fifth regiment, the 6th U.S. Cavalry, had been sent to Fairfield earlier that morning, where it fought its devastating battle with Virginia cavalry.

Merritt dismounted most of his troopers and sent out skirmishers against Brig. Gen. Evander Law's Brigade (Longstreet's Corps), which was defending that part of the flank west of the Emmitsburg Road. Stubborn Confederate resistance convinced Merritt to pull them back after about thirty minutes of fighting. The area of the skirmish, known today as South Cavalry Field, is shown at the top of the opposite facing page in a photograph dating from the 1940s.

About one-half mile farther east, a brigade of Brig. Gen. H. Judson Kilpatrick's Third Division of cavalry under Brig. Gen. Elon J. Farnsworth took position on Bushman's Hill near Big Round Top. Like Merritt, Kilpatrick planned to attack the

(NATIONAL PARK SERVICE)

Confederate flank, but he intended to make his assault with mounted horsemen.

After sending two of his regiments in failed mounted attacks against the skirmish line of the 1st Texas and 47th Alabama infantry, Kilpatrick ordered Farnsworth to lead a mounted assault with the 1st Vermont Cavalry. The sloping ground and large boulders broke up the charge, which is depicted on a bronze tablet (shown below) on the front of the monument at the foot of Bushman's Hill dedicated to Maj. William Wells of the 1st Vermont Cavalry, who earned the Medal of Honor for leading part of the charge.

July 3 - 5:30 to 6:00 p.m.: Farnsworth Charges the Confederate Line

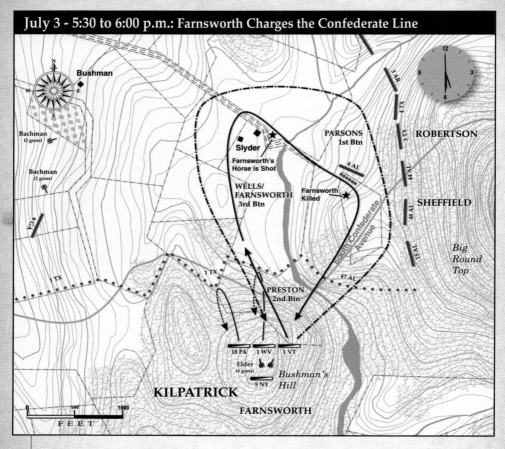

Farnsworth led the 600 men of the 1st Vermont Cavalry down the hill, into the Confederate skirmish line, and behind the enemy defenses, where they were hammered by Confederate artillery posted to the northwest. Many of the Vermonters came under musket fire from Texas and Alabama regiments when they turned east. Farnsworth was shot off his horse and died a few moments later in an open farm field at the western base of Little Round Top. Farnsworth's Charge, as it is known today, accomplished nothing except to add to the death toll. It was the final attack at Gettysburg.

The third and final day of combat at Gettysburg, a day of indescribable death, sacrifice, determination, and bravery, was finally over. The Confederate attempt to score a decisive victory on Northern soil had failed.

The Retreat from Gettysburg

A thunderstorm rolled over the battlefield a few hours after Pickett's Charge receded from Cemetery Ridge. The rain may have begun to wash some of the blood from the field, but nothing could reverse the horrific damage suffered by both armies during the three-day battle.

Lee's Army of Northern Virginia was no longer capable of remaining on the field. Losses across the board were simply staggering. In all, Lee lost more than 23,000 of some 75,000 men (nearly 30% losses). Nearly seven of ten officers (4,700 of 6,900) had been killed, wounded, or captured.

The price paid for victory by George Meade's Army of the Potomac was likewise heavy. Federal casualties were in excess of 23,000, nearly 25% of his army. Meade lost more than 3,100 of his 7,000 officers to all causes, a loss of 45%. By the end of July 3, nearly 50,000 Americans (Confederate and Federal combined) had been killed, mortally wounded, wounded, or were captured/missing.

Low on ammunition and food and with his ranks decimated, Lee had no choice but to give up the field and slip his battered army south to Virginia as quickly as possible. The attempt proved to be a logistical nightmare with more than 70 miles of uneven road, some winding through mountains, separating the defeated army from the Potomac River. In addition, thousands of wounded needed to be transported in a wagon train stretching 17 miles, with thousands of Federal prisoners to watch over at the same time. There was also the matter of a strong Federal army less than one mile away across the corpse-strewn field. Would Meade allow his enemy to retreat unmolested?

(BATTLES AND LEADERS)

Lee began preparations to leave the field late on July 3. In the early morning hours of July 4 – Independence Day – hundreds of army wagons were pressed into service as ambulances. Most of the wounded were moved west along the road to Cashtown and then south for Hagerstown, Maryland, and the river crossing at Williamsport. Lee's main army began marching southwest toward Fairfield and then south for the crossings at Williamsport and Falling Waters. The steady rain turned the roads into a muddy gruel, making the march even more miserable as depicted in the *Battles and Leaders* engraving above.

(LIBRARY OF CONGRESS)

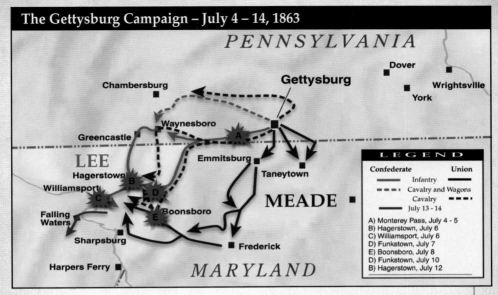

The Gettysburg Campaign – July 4 – 14, 1863

PENNSYLVANIA

Dover

Gettysburg

Chambersburg

Wrightsville

York

Waynesboro

Greencastle

Emmitsburg

Taneytown

LEE

Hagerstown

Williamsport

B

D

MEADE

Falling
Waters

C

E

Boonsboro

Sharpsburg

Frederick

Harpers Ferry

MARYLAND

LEGEND

Confederate		Union
———	Infantry	
– – – –	Cavalry and Wagons	
	Cavalry	– – – –
	July 13 - 14	

A) Monterey Pass, July 4 - 5
B) Hagerstown, July 6
C) Williamsport, July 6
D) Funkstown, July 7
E) Boonsboro, July 8
D) Funkstown, July 10
B) Hagerstown, July 12

While his wounded and army retreated along the two main routes, a covering force consisting of part of Ewell's Second Corps and some cavalry remained behind. Meade wasn't sure if the Confederates were in full retreat until as late as the morning of July 5. On the previous evening, Maj. Gen. Judson Kilpatrick's Federal cavalry division attacked Confederate supply wagons heading south through the Monterey Pass south of Fairfield (about ten miles southwest of Gettysburg). Kilpatrick burned dozens of the wagons and corralled a number of prisoners.

On July 5, Meade began what some have called a half-hearted pursuit of the Southern army. Maj. Gen. John Sedgwick's VI Corps marched along the Fairfield Road and skirmished briefly with Ewell's rearguard. In the painting at the bottom of the previous page, artist Edwin Forbes depicts Federal troops marching south near Emmitsburg, Maryland, as the rain continued to pour.

On July 6 at Hagerstown, Maryland, Kilpatrick's cavalry engaged Confederate cavalry and infantry but was eventually driven from the town. One of his brigade commanders, Brig. Gen. George A. Custer, used the cupola of the Zion Reformed Church (right) as an observation post. The door is the same one that stood in 1863.

RETREAT FROM GETTYSB

Lee paroled a number of Federal prisoners (especially the wounded) on the field before retreating, but took several thousand with him on the long slog south to Virginia. Meade sent his Confederate prisoners, estimated at more than 5,000, under guard to Taneytown, Maryland, for further processing. Many of the captives, represented at left in an Alfred Waud drawing marching in an enormous column, ended up at Fort Delaware. By the following month that prison housed more than 12,000 prisoners.

By July 7, Meade's entire army was in pursuit of the fleeing Rebels. From then until July 12, however, the opposing cavalry forces bore the brunt of the fighting in and around the Maryland towns of Funkstown, Boonsboro, Williamsport, and again at Hagerstown. J.E.B. Stuart and his Southern troopers masterfully fought off the generally uncoordinated attacks by Federal cavalry and kept them from gaining Lee's rear and cutting off his progress to the Potomac River.

Lee's engineers, meanwhile, were busy constructing miles of formidable defensive works along Salisbury Ridge (depicted in the Edwin Forbes painting at top of opposite facing page). Infantry, cavalry, and artillery manned the works to protect the critical river crossings behind them (to their west).

Many of the Union soldiers along the Federal line to the east, less than a mile away from the Confederate defenses, knew their opportunity to attack and defeat Lee's army was slipping rapidly away. The heavy rains that fell after the Gettysburg battle swelled

(LIBRARY OF CONGRESS)

the Potomac, hindering the Rebels' ability to cross it to safety. The weather began to improve by July 11 and the water level started to drop. On the night of July 12, General Meade called a council of war with his corps commanders to determine whether to attack Lee's strong entrenchments. Meade wanted to attack the next day, but his officers were divided. A few voted to attack, but most wished to wait at least one more day. Meade decided against an attack on July 13. Other than some desultory skirmishing along the lines, both armies spent that day waiting for fighting that never occurred.

Lee's pontoon bridge across the river at Falling Waters was ready that night and he began crossing his army there and at Williamsport under the cover of darkness. Ewell's Corps waded the river at Williamsport and Longstreet's and Hill's soldiers, plus most of the Southern cavalry, crossed the river on the bridge at Falling Waters. When the sun rose the next morning, the Federals discovered that most of the Confederates were gone. An audacious attack by Gen. George Custer's 6th Michigan Cavalry (bottom of opposite facing page) against Maj. Gen. Henry Heth's rearguard at Falling Waters accomplished nothing. Robert E. Lee, nicknamed the "Gray Fox" by many in the Union Army, had successfully slipped his men away.

Pictured to the right is a small cascading waterfall on the West Virginia side of the Potomac River that gives the Falling Waters crossing its name.

The Alfred Waud drawing above depicts Lt. Gen. Richard Ewell's Corps wading the Potomac at the Williamsport crossing. Because the water was still high on the night of July 13, the men waded cautiously through water chest-deep. Lee's wagons of wounded also crossed here on a ferry that was worked around the clock for several days.

Over the following week Meade constructed pontoon bridges to cross the Potomac River and continue the pursuit. The photograph below, titled "Leisurely Pursuit," was taken on July 21, 1863. It depicts the bridges near Berlin, Maryland. President Abraham Lincoln lauded the Gettysburg victory but was very frustrated that Meade was unable to cut off and destroy Lee's army before they escaped.

The Southern defeat at Gettysburg, combined with the loss of Vicksburg, Mississippi, was a serious double blow to the Confederate cause. The Southern armies marched and fought for nearly two more long years until the final surrenders in April and May of 1865.

(MILLERS PHOTOGRAPHIC HISTORY OF THE CIVIL WAR)

Order of Battle, July 1 - 3, 1863

The Order of Battle for the July 1-3 combat at Gettysburg is available from a wide variety of sources, but as discerning students discover, these often vary. What follows is based upon years of careful research in original archival sources. We think (and hope) they are the most complete and accurate to date, and that you find them useful.

The following designations are used to denote casualties:

(w) = wounded

(c) = captured

(mw) = mortally wounded

(k) = killed

When identified subordinate officers took command for wounded commanders, they are listed in descending order. Sometimes, due to incomplete records (especially on the Confederate side), it is impossible to determine who assumed command.

Battle of Gettysburg, Pa., July 1-3

FEDERAL FORCES

ARMY OF THE POTOMAC
Maj. Gen. George G. Meade, Commanding

ARMY HEADQUARTERS
Maj. Gen. Daniel Butterfield, Chief of Staff (w)
Brig. Gen. Gouverneur K. Warren, Chief of Engineers (w)
Brig. Gen. Henry J. Hunt, Chief of Artillery
Brig. Gen. Seth Williams, Assistant Adjutant General
Lt. Col. Joseph Dickinson, Adjutant General Staff (w)
Brig. Gen. Rufus Ingalls, Chief Quartermaster
Col. Edmund Schriver, Inspector General
Dr. Jonathan Letterman, Medical Director
Col. George H. Sharpe, Bureau of Military Information
Lt. John R. Edie, Acting Chief Ordnance Officer (acting)

Provost Marshal
Brig. Gen. Marsena R. Patrick

93rd New York Infantry
Col. John S. Crocker

8th United States Infantry (eight companies)
Capt. Edwin W. H. Read

2nd Pennsylvania Cavalry
Col. R. Butler Price

6th Pennsylvania Cavalry, Companies E and I
Capt. James Starr
Cavalry detachments from 1st, 2nd, 5th,
and 6th Regiments United States Cavalry

Headquarters Guards and Orderlies
Oneida (New York) Cavalry
Capt. Daniel P. Mann

Signal Corps
Capt. Lemuel B. Norton

Engineer Brigade
Brig. Gen. Henry W. Benham

15th New York Engineers (three companies)
Maj. Walter L. Cassin

50th New York Engineers
Col. William H. Pettes

United States Engineer Battalion
Capt. George H. Mendell

I ARMY CORPS
Maj. Gen. John F. Reynolds (k)
Maj. Gen. Abner Doubleday (relieved from corps command)
Maj. Gen. John Newton

Headquarters Guards and Orderlies

1st Maine Cavalry, Company L
Capt. Constantine Taylor

FIRST DIVISION
Brig. Gen. James S. Wadsworth

First Brigade ("Iron Brigade")
Brig. Gen. Solomon Meredith (w)
Col. William W. Robinson

19th Indiana
Col. Samuel J. Williams

24th Michigan
Col. Henry A. Morrow (w)
Capt. Albert M. Edwards

2d Wisconsin
Col. Lucius Fairchild (w)
Maj. John Mansfield (w)
Capt. George H. Otis

6th Wisconsin
Lt. Col. Rufus R. Dawes

7th Wisconsin
Col. William W. Robinson
Lt. Col. John B. Callis (w-c)
Maj. Mark Finnicum

Second Brigade
Brig. Gen. Lysander Cutler

7th Indiana
Col. Ira G. Grover

76th New York
Maj. Andrew J. Grover (k)
Capt. John E. Cook

84th New York (14th Brooklyn)
Col. Edward B. Fowler

95th New York
Col. George H. Biddle (w)
Maj. Edward Pye

147th New York
Lt. Col. Francis C. Miller (w)
Maj. George Harney

56th Pennsylvania (9 companies)
Col. J. William Hofmann

SECOND DIVISION
Brig. Gen. John C. Robinson

First Brigade
Brig. Gen. Gabriel R. Paul (w)
Col. Samuel H. Leonard (w)
Col. Adrian R. Root (w-c)
Col. Richard Coulter (final command of brigade)
Col. Peter Lyle

16th Maine
Col. Charles W. Tilden (c)
Maj. Archibald D. Leavitt

13th Massachusetts
Col. Samuel H. Leonard (w)
Lt. Col. N. Walter Batchelder

94th New York
Col. Adrian R. Root (w-c)
Maj. Samuel A. Moffett

104th New York
Col. Gilbert G. Prey

107th Pennsylvania
Lt. Col. James MacThomson (w)
Capt. Emanuel D. Roath

Second Brigade
Brig. Gen. Henry Baxter

12th Massachusetts
Col. James L. Bates (w)
Lt. Col. David Allen, Jr.

83d New York (9th New York Militia)
Lt. Col. Joseph A. Moesch

97th New York
Col. Charles Wheelock (w-c)
Maj. Charles Northrup

11th Pennsylvania
Col. Richard Coulter (w)
Capt. Benjamin F. Haines (w)
Capt. John B. Overmyer

88th Pennsylvania
Maj. Benezet F. Foust (w)
Capt. Edmund A. Mass (c)
Capt. Henry Whiteside

90th Pennsylvania
Col. Peter Lyle (final command of regiment
after temporarily commanding brigade)
Maj. Alfred J. Sellers

THIRD DIVISION
Maj. Gen. Abner Doubleday (final command after being relieved of corps command)
Brig. Gen. Thomas A. Rowley

First Brigade
Col. Chapman Biddle
(w – final command of brigade)
Brig. Gen. Thomas A. Rowley

80th New York (20th New York Militia)
Col. Theodore B. Gates

121st Pennsylvania
Col. Chapman Biddle (w)
Maj. Alexander Biddle

142d Pennsylvania
Col. Robert P. Cummins (mw)
Lt. Col. A. B. McCalmont

151st Pennsylvania
Lt. Col. George F. McFarland (w)
Capt. Walter L. Owens
Col. Harrison Allen

Second Brigade
Col. Roy Stone (w)
Col. Langhorne Wister (w)
Col. Edmund L. Dana

143d Pennsylvania
Col. Edmund L. Dana
Lt. Col. John D. Musser

149th Pennsylvania
Lt. Col. Walton Dwight (w)
Capt. James Glenn

150th Pennsylvania
Col. Langhorne Wister (w)
Lt. Col. Henry S. Huidekoper (w)
Capt. Cornelius C. Widdis

Third Brigade
Brig. Gen. George J. Stannard (w)
Col. Francis V. Randall

12th Vermont (detached as train guard)
Col. Asa P. Blunt

13th Vermont
Col. Francis V. Randall
Lt. Col. William D. Munson
(final command of regiment)
Maj. Joseph J. Boynton

14th Vermont
Col. William T. Nichols

15th Vermont (detached as train guard)
Col. Redfield Proctor

16th Vermont
Col. Wheelock G. Veazey

Artillery Brigade
Col. Charles S. Wainright

2nd Maine Light Artillery,
Battery B (Six 3-inch Ordnance Rifles)
Capt. James A. Hall

5th Maine Light Artillery,
Battery E (Six Napoleons)
Capt. Greenleaf T. Stevens (w)
Lt. Edward N. Whittier

1st New York Light Artillery, Batteries
L and E (Six 3-inch Ordnance Rifles)
Capt. Gilbert H. Reynolds (w)
Lt. George Breck

1st Pennsylvania Light Artillery,
Battery B (Four 3-inch Ordnance Rifles)
Capt. James H. Cooper

4th United States Light Artillery,
Battery B (Six Napoleons)
Lt. James Stewart

II ARMY CORPS

Maj. Gen. Winfield S. Hancock (w)
Brig. Gen. John Gibbon (w)
Brig. Gen. John C. Caldwell
Brig. Gen. William Hays

Headquarters Guards and Orderlies

6th New York Cavalry, Companies D and K
Lt. Henry A. Wetmore

FIRST DIVISION

Brig. Gen. John C. Caldwell

Provost Guard

Provost Marshal
Lt. William M. Hobart (116th Pennsylvania)

116th Pennsylvania, Company B

53rd Pennsylvania, Companies A, B and K

First Brigade
Col. Edward E. Cross (mw)
Col. H. Boyd McKeen

5th New Hampshire
Lt. Col. Charles E. Hapgood

61st New York
Lt. Col. K. Oscar Broady

81st Pennsylvania
Col. H. Boyd McKeen
Lt. Col. Amos Stroh

148th Pennsylvania
Lt. Col. Robert McFarlane

Second Brigade ("Irish Brigade")
Col. Patrick Kelly

28th Massachusetts
Col. Richard Byrnes

63d New York (2 companies)
Lt. Col. Richard C. Bentley (w)
Capt. Thomas Touhy

69th New York (2 companies)
Capt. Richard Moroney (w)
Lt. James J. Smith

88th New York (2 companies)
Capt. Denis F. Burke

116th Pennsylvania (3 companies)
Maj. St. Clair A. Mulholland

Third Brigade
Brig. Gen. Samuel K. Zook (mw)
Lt. Col. John Fraser

52d New York
Lt. Col. Charles G. Freudenberg (w)
Capt. William Scherrer

57th New York
Lt. Col. Alford B. Chapman

66th New York
Col. Orlando H. Morris (w)
Lt. Col. John S. Hammell (w)
Maj. Peter Nelson

140th Pennsylvania
Col. Richard P. Roberts (k)
Lt. Col. John Fraser

Fourth Brigade
Col. John R. Brooke (w)

27th Connecticut (2 companies)
Lt. Col. Henry C. Merwin (k)
Maj. James H. Coburn

2d Delaware
Col. William P. Baily
Capt. Charles H. Christman

64th New York
Col. Daniel G. Bingham (w)
Maj. Leman W. Bradley

53d Pennsylvania
Lt. Col. Richard McMichael

145th Pennsylvania (7 companies)
Col. Hiram L. Brown (w)
Capt. John W. Reynolds (w)
Capt. Moses W. Oliver

SECOND DIVISION
Brig. Gen. John Gibbon (w)
Brig. Gen. William Harrow

Provost Guard

1st Minnesota, Company C

First Brigade
Brig. Gen. William Harrow
Col. Francis E. Heath

19th Maine
Col. Francis E. Heath
Lt. Col. Henry W. Cunningham

15th Massachusetts
Col. George H. Ward (mw)
Lt. Col. George C. Joslin

1st Minnesota (2nd Company Minnesota
Sharpshooters attached)
Col. William Colvill, Jr. (w)
Capt. Nathan S. Messick (k)
Capt. Henry C. Coates

82d New York (2nd New York Militia)
Lt. Col. James Huston (k)
Capt. John Darrow

Second Brigade
Brig. Gen. Alexander S. Webb (w)

69th Pennsylvania
Col. Dennis O'Kane (mw)
Capt. William Davis

71st Pennsylvania
Col. Richard Penn Smith

72d Pennsylvania
Col. De Witt C. Baxter (w)
Lt. Col. Theodore Hesser

106th Pennsylvania
Lt. Col. William L. Curry

Third Brigade
Col. Norman J. Hall

19th Massachusetts
Col. Arthur F. Devereux

20th Massachusetts
Col. Paul J. Revere (mw)
Lt. Col. George N. Macy (w)
Capt. Henry L. Abbott.

7th Michigan
Lt. Col. Amos E. Steele, Jr. (k)
Maj. Sylvanus W. Curtis

42d New York
Col. James E. Mallon

59th New York (4 companies)
Lieut. Col. Max A. Thoman (mw)
Capt. William McFadden

Unattached

1st Massachusetts Sharpshooters
Capt. William Plumer
Lt. Emerson L. Bicknell

THIRD DIVISION
Brig. Gen. Alexander Hays

Provost Guard

10th New York Battalion
Maj. George F. Hopper

First Brigade
Col. Samuel S. Carroll

14th Indiana
Col. John Coons

4th Ohio
Lt. Col. Leonard W. Carpenter

8th Ohio
Lt. Col. Franklin Sawyer

7th West Virginia
Lt. Col. Jonathan H. Lockwood

Second Brigade
Col. Thomas A. Smyth (w)
Lt. Col. Francis E. Pierce

14th Connecticut
Maj. Theodore G. Ellis

1st Delaware
Lt. Col. Edward P. Harris
Capt. Thomas B. Hizar (w)
Lt. William Smith (mw)
Lt. John T. Dent

12th New Jersey
Maj. John T. Hill

108th New York
Lt. Col. Francis E. Pierce

Third Brigade
Col. George L. Willard (k)
Col. Eliakim Sherrill (mw)
Col. Clinton D. MacDougall (w)
Lt. Col. James L. Bull

39th New York (4 companies)
Maj. Hugo Hildebrandt (w)

111th New York
Col. Clinton D. MacDougall (w)
Lt. Col. Isaac M. Lusk (w)
Capt. Aaron P. Seeley

125th New York
Lt. Col. Levin Crandell

126th New York
Col. Eliakim Sherrill (mw)
Lt. Col. James L. Bull
Capt. Morris Brown

Artillery Brigade
Capt. John G. Hazard

1st New York Light Artillery,
Battery B and 14th New York Light Artillery
(Four 10-Pounder Parrotts)
Lt. Albert S. Sheldon (w)
Capt. James McKay Rorty (k)
Lt. Robert E. Rogers

1st Rhode Island Light Artillery,
Battery A (Six 3-inch Ordnance Rifles)
Capt. William A. Arnold

1st Rhode Island Light Artillery,
Battery B (Six 3-inch Ordnance Rifles)
Lt. T. Fred Brown (w)
Lt. Walter S. Perrin

1st United States Light Artillery,
Battery I (Six Napoleons)
Lt. George A. Woodruff (mw)
Lt. Tully McCrea

4th United States Light Artillery,
Battery A (Six 3-inch Ordnance Rifles)
Lt. Alonzo H. Cushing (k)
Sgt. Frederick Fuger

III ARMY CORPS
Maj. Gen. Daniel E. Sickles (w)
Maj. Gen. David B. Birney

Headquarters Guards and Orderlies

6th New York Cavalry, Company A

9th New York Cavalry, Companies F and K (attached July 2 only)
Capt. Timothy Hanley

FIRST DIVISION
Maj. Gen. David B. Birney
Brig. Gen. J. H. Hobart Ward

First Brigade
Brig. Gen. Charles K. Graham (w-c)
Col. Andrew H. Tippin

57th Pennsylvania (8 companies)
Col. Peter Sides (w)
Capt. Alanson H. Nelson

63d Pennsylvania
Maj. John A. Danks

68th Pennsylvania
Col. Andrew H. Tippin
Capt. Milton S. Davis

105th Pennsylvania
Col. Calvin A. Craig

114th Pennsylvania (Collis' Zouaves)
Lt. Col. Frederick F. Cavada (c)
Capt. Edward R. Bowen

141st Pennsylvania
Col. Henry J. Madill

Second Brigade
Brig. Gen. J. H. Hobart Ward
Col. Hiram Berdan

20th Indiana
Col. John Wheeler (k)
Lt. Col. William C. L. Taylor (w)

3d Maine
Col. Moses B. Lakeman

4th Maine
Col. Elijah Walker (w)
Capt. Edwin Libby

86th New York
Lt. Col. Benjamin L. Higgins

124th New York
Col. A. Van Horne Ellis (k)
Lt. Col. Francis M. Cummins
(final command of regiment)
Capt. Charles Weygant

99th Pennsylvania
Maj. John W. Moore

1st United States Sharpshooters
Col. Hiram Berdan
Lt. Col. Casper Trepp

2nd United States Sharpshooters
(8 companies)
Maj. Homer R. Stoughton

Third Brigade
Col. P. Regis de Trobriand

17th Maine
Lt. Col. Charles B. Merrill

3d Michigan
Col. Byron R. Pierce (w)
Lt. Col. Edwin S. Pierce

5th Michigan
Lt. Col. John Pulford (w)
Maj. Salmon S. Matthews (w)
Lt. Charles T. Bissell

40th New York
Col. Thomas W. Egan (w)

110th Pennsylvania (6 companies)
Lt. Col. David M. Jones (w)
Maj. Isaac Rogers

SECOND DIVISION
Brig. Gen. Andrew A. Humphreys

First Brigade
Brig. Gen. Joseph B. Karr

1st Massachusetts
Lt. Col. Clark B. Baldwin (w)

11th Massachusetts
Lt. Col. Porter D. Tripp

16th Massachusetts
Lt. Col. Waldo Merriam (w)
Capt. Matthew Donovan

12th New Hampshire
Capt. John F. Langley

11th New Jersey
Col. Robert McAllister (w)
Capt. Luther Martin (w)
Lt. John Schoonover (w)
(final command of regiment)
Capt. William H. Lloyd (w)
Capt. Samuel T. Sleeper

26th Pennsylvania
Maj. Robert L. Bodine

84th Pennsylvania
(detached, guarding Corps trains)
Lt. Col. Milton Opp

Second Brigade
Col. William R. Brewster

70th New York
Col. J. Egbert Farnum

71st New York
Col. Henry L. Potter (w)

72d New York
Col. John S. Austin (w)
Lt. Col. John Leonard

73d New York
Maj. Michael W. Burns

74th New York
Lt. Col. Thomas Holt

120th New York
Lt. Col. Cornelius D. Westbrook (w)
Maj. John R. Tappen

Third Brigade
Col. George C. Burling

2d New Hampshire
Col. Edward L. Bailey

5th New Jersey
Col. William J. Sewell (w)
Capt. Thomas C. Godfrey
Capt. Henry H. Woolsey (w)
(final command of regiment)

6th New Jersey
Lt. Col. Stephen R. Gilkyson

7th New Jersey
Col. Louis R. Francine (mw)
Maj. Frederick Cooper

8th New Jersey
Col. John Ramsey (w)
Capt. John G. Langston

115th Pennsylvania
Maj. John P. Dunne

Artillery Brigade
Capt. George E. Randolph (w)
Capt. A. Judson Clark

1st New Jersey Light Artillery,
2nd Battery (B)
(Six 10-pounder Parrotts)
Capt. A. Judson Clark
Lt. Robert Sims

1st New York Light Artillery,
Battery D (Six Napoleons)
Capt. George B. Winslow

New York Light Artillery,
4th Battery (Six 10-pounder Parrotts)
Capt. James E. Smith

1st Rhode Island Light Artillery,
Battery E (Six Napoleons)
Lt. John K. Bucklyn (w)
Lt. Benjamin Freeborn (w)

4th United States Light Artillery,
Battery K (Six Napoleons)
Lt. Francis W. Seeley (w)
Lt. Robert James

V ARMY CORPS
Maj. Gen. George Sykes

Provost Guard

12th New York Infantry, Companies D and E
Capt. Henry W. Rider

Headquarters Guard and Orderlies

17th Pennsylvania Cavalry, Companies D and H
Capt. William Thompson

FIRST DIVISION
Brig. Gen. James Barnes (w)

First Brigade
Col. William S. Tilton

18th Massachusetts
Col. Joseph Hayes (w)

22nd Massachusetts,
2nd Company Massachusetts Sharpshooters
(attached to regiment)
Lt. Col. Thomas Sherwin, Jr.

1st Michigan
Col. Ira C. Abbott (w)
Lt. Col. William A. Throop (w)

118th Pennsylvania
Lt. Col. James Gwyn

Second Brigade
Col. Jacob B. Sweitzer

9th Massachusetts
Col. Patrick R. Guiney

32nd Massachusetts (9 companies)
Col. George L. Prescott

4th Michigan
Col. Harrison H. Jeffords (mw)
Lt. Col. George W. Lumbard

62nd Pennsylvania
Lt. Col. James C. Hull

Third Brigade
Col. Strong Vincent (mw)
Col. James C. Rice

20th Maine
Col. Joshua L. Chamberlain

16th Michigan,
1st Company Michigan Sharpshooters
(attached to regiment)
Lt. Col. Norval E. Welch

44th New York
Col. James C. Rice
Lt. Col. Freeman Conner

83d Pennsylvania
Capt. Orpheus S. Woodward

SECOND DIVISION
Brig. Gen. Romeyn B. Ayers

First Brigade
Col. Hannibal Day

3rd United States (6 companies)
Capt. Henry W. Freedley
Capt. Richard G. Lay

4th United States (4 companies)
Capt. Julius W. Adams, Jr.

6th United States (5 companies)
Capt. Levi C. Bootes

12th United States (8 companies)
Capt. Thomas S. Dunn

14th United States (8 companies)
Maj. Grotius R. Giddings

Second Brigade
Col. Sidney Burbank

2nd United States (6 companies)
Maj. Arthur T. Lee (w)
Capt. Samuel A. McKee

7th United States (4 companies)
Capt. David P. Hancock

10th United States (3 companies)
Capt. William Clinton

11th United States (6 companies)
Maj. DeLancey Floyd-Jones

17th United States (7 companies)
Lt. Col. J. Durell Greene

Third Brigade
Brig. Gen. Stephen H. Weed (k)
Col. Kenner Garrard

140th New York
Col. Patrick H. O'Rorke (k)
Lt. Col. Louis Ernst

146th New York
Col. Kenner Garrard
Lt. Col. David T. Jenkins

91st Pennsylvania
Lt. Col. Joseph H. Sinex

155th Pennsylvania
Lt. Col. John H. Cain

THIRD DIVISION
Brig. Gen. Samuel W. Crawford

First Brigade
Col. William McCandless

1st Pennsylvania Reserves (9 companies)
Col. William C. Talley

2nd Pennsylvania Reserves (9 companies)
Lt. Col. George A. Woodward

6th Pennsylvania Reserves
Lt. Col. Wellington H. Ent

13th Pennsylvania Reserves
Col. Charles F. Taylor (k)
Maj. William R. Hartshorne

Third Brigade
Col. Joseph W. Fisher

5th Pennsylvania Reserves
Lt. Col. George Dare

9th Pennsylvania Reserves
Lt. Col. James McK. Snodgrass

10th Pennsylvania Reserves
Col. Adoniram J. Warner

11th Pennsylvania Reserves
Col. Samuel M. Jackson

12th Pennsylvania Reserves (9 companies)
Col. Martin D. Hardin

Artillery Brigade
Capt. Augustus P. Martin

Massachusetts Light Artillery,
3rd Battery (C) (Six Napoleons)
Lt. Aaron F. Walcott

1st New York Light Artillery,
Battery C (Four 3-inch Ordnance Rifles)
Capt. Almont Barnes

1st Ohio Light Artillery,
Battery L (Six Napoleons)
Capt. Frank C. Gibbs

5th United States Light Artillery,
Battery D (Six 10-pounder Parrotts)
Lt. Charles E. Hazlett (k)
Lt. Benjamin F. Rittenhouse

5th United States Light Artillery,
Battery I (Four 3-inch Ordnance Rifles)
Lt. Malbone F. Watson (w)
Lt. Charles C. MacConnell

VI ARMY CORPS
Maj. Gen. John Sedgwick

Provost Guard

1st Massachusetts Cavalry
Lt. Greely S. Curtis

Headquarters Guard and Orderlies

1st New Jersey Cavalry, Company L and 1st Pennsylvania Cavalry, Company H
Capt. William S. Craft

FIRST DIVISION
Brig. Gen. Horatio G. Wright

Provost Guard

4th New Jersey (3 companies)
Capt. William R. Maxwell

First Brigade
Brig. Gen. Alfred T. A. Torbert

1st New Jersey
Lt. Col. William Henry, Jr.

2nd New Jersey
Lt. Col. Charles Wiebecke

3rd New Jersey
Col. Henry W. Brown

15th New Jersey
Col. William H. Penrose

Second Brigade
Brig. Gen. Joseph J. Bartlett

5th Maine
Col. Clark S. Edwards

121st New York
Col. Emory Upton

95th Pennsylvania
Lt. Col. Edward Carroll

96th Pennsylvania
Maj. William H. Lessig

Third Brigade
Brig. Gen. David A. Russell

6th Maine
Col. Hiram Burnham

49th Pennsylvania (4 companies)
Lt. Col. Thomas M. Hulings

119th Pennsylvania
Col. Peter C. Ellmaker

5th Wisconsin
Col. Thomas S. Allen

SECOND DIVISION
Brig. Gen. Albion P. Howe

Second Brigade
Col. Lewis A. Grant

2d Vermont
Col. James H. Walbridge

3d Vermont
Col. Thomas O. Seaver

4th Vermont
Col. Charles B. Stoughton

5th Vermont
Lt. Col. John R. Lewis

6th Vermont
Col. Elisha L. Barney

Third Brigade
Brig. Gen. Thomas H. Neill

7th Maine (6 companies)
Lt. Col. Selden Connor

43rd New York
Lt. Col. John Wilson

49th New York
Col. Daniel D. Bidwell

33rd New York (attached to 49th New York)
Capt. Henry J. Gifford

77th New York
Lt. Col. Winsor B. French

61st Pennsylvania
Lt. Col. George F. Smith

THIRD DIVISION
Maj. Gen. John Newton
Brig. Gen. Frank Wheaton

First Brigade
Brig. Gen. Alexander Shaler

65th New York
Col. Joseph E. Hamblin

67th New York
Col. Nelson Cross

122nd New York
Col. Silas Titus

23rd Pennsylvania
Lt. Col. John F. Glenn

82nd Pennsylvania
Col. Isaac C. Bassett

Second Brigade
Col. Henry L. Eustis

7th Massachusetts
Lt. Col. Franklin P. Harlow

10th Massachusetts
Lt. Col. Joseph B. Parsons

37th Massachusetts
Col. Oliver Edwards

2nd Rhode Island
Col. Horatio Rogers, Jr.

Third Brigade
Brig. Gen. Frank Wheaton
Col. David J. Nevin

62nd New York
Col. David J. Nevin
Lt. Col. Theodore B. Hamilton

93rd Pennsylvania
Maj. John I. Nevin

98th Pennsylvania
Maj. John B. Kohler

102nd Pennsylvania (detached guarding
wagons at Westminster, MD)
Col. John W. Patterson

139th Pennsylvania
Col. Frederick H. Collier (w)
Lt. Col. William H. Moody

Artillery Brigade
Col. Charles H. Tompkins

Massachusetts Light Artillery,
1st Battery (A) (Six Napoleons)
Capt. William H. McCartney

New York Light Artillery,
1st Battery (Six 3-inch Ordnance Rifles)
Capt. Andrew Cowan

New York Light Artillery,
3rd Battery (Six 10-pounder Parrotts)
Capt. William A. Harn

1st Rhode Island Light Artillery,
Battery C (Six 3-inch Ordnance Rifles)
Capt. Richard Waterman

1st Rhode Island Light Artillery,
Battery G (Six 10-pounder Parrotts)
Capt. George W. Adams

2nd United States Light Artillery,
Battery D (Six Napoleons)
Lt. Edward B. Williston

2nd United States Light Artillery,
Battery G (Six Napoleons)
Lt. John H. Butler

5th United States Light Artillery,
Battery F (Six 10-pounder Parrotts)
Lt. Leonard Martin

XI ARMY CORPS
Maj. Gen. Oliver O. Howard (final command of corps)
Maj. Gen. Carl Schurz

Headquarters Guard and Orderlies

1st Indiana Cavalry, Companies I and K
Capt. Abram Sharra

17th Pennsylvania Cavalry, Company K
Capt. Richard Fitzgerald

8th New York Infantry (1 company)
Lt. Hermann Foerster

FIRST DIVISION
Brig. Gen. Francis C. Barlow (w-c)
Brig. Gen. Adelbert Ames

First Brigade
Col. Leopold Von Gilsa

41st New York (9 companies)
Lt. Col. Detleo von Einsiedel

54th New York
Maj. Stephen Kovacs (c)
Lt. Ernst Both

68th New York
Col. Gotthilf Bourry

153rd Pennsylvania
Maj. John F. Frueauff

Second Brigade
Brig. Gen. Adelbert Ames
Col. Andrew L. Harris

17th Connecticut
Lt. Col. Douglas Fowler (k)
Maj. Allen G. Brady

25th Ohio
Lt. Col. Jeremiah Williams (c)
Capt. Nathaniel J. Manning (w)
Lt. William Maloney
Lt. Israel White

75th Ohio
Col. Andrew L. Harris
Capt. George B. Fox

107th Ohio
Col. Seraphim Meyer (w)
Capt. John M. Lutz

SECOND DIVISION
Brig. Gen. Adolph von Steinwehr

Provost Guard
29th New York Independent Company

First Brigade
Col. Charles R. Coster

134th New York
Lt. Col. Allan H. Jackson

154th New York
Lt. Col. Daniel B. Allen

27th Pennsylvania
Lt. Col. Lorenz Cantador

73rd Pennsylvania
Capt. Daniel F. Kelley

Second Brigade
Col. Orland Smith

33d Massachusetts
Col. Adin B. Underwood

136th New York
Col. James Wood, Jr.

55th Ohio
Col. Charles B. Gambee

73d Ohio
Lt. Col. Richard Long

THIRD DIVISION
Maj. Gen. Carl Schurz (final command of division)
Brig. Gen. Alexander Schimmelfennig (m)

First Brigade
Brig. Gen. Alexander Schimmelfennig (m)
Col. George von Amsberg

82nd Illinois
Lt. Col. Edward S. Salomon

45th New York
Col. George von Amsberg
Lt. Col. Adolphus Dobke

157th New York
Col. Philip B. Brown, Jr.

61st Ohio
Col. Stephen J. McGroarty

74th Pennsylvania
Col. Adolph von Hartung (w)
Lt. Col. Alexander von Mitzel (c)
Capt. Gustav Schleiter
Capt. Henry Krauseneck

Second Brigade
Col. Wladimir Krzyzanowski

58th New York
Lt. Col. August Otto
Capt. Emil Koenig

119th New York
Col. John T. Lockman (w)
Lt. Col. Edward F. Lloyd

82d Ohio
Col. James S. Robinson (w)
Lt. Col. David Thomson

75th Pennsylvania
Col. Francis Mahler (mw)
Maj. August Ledig

26th Wisconsin
Lt. Col. Hans Boebel (w)
Capt. John W. Fuchs

Artillery Brigade
Maj. Thomas W. Osborn

1st New York Light Artillery,
Battery I (Six 3-inch Ordnance Rifles)
Capt. Michael Wiedrich

New York Light Artillery,
13th Battery (Four 3-inch Ordnance Rifles)
Lt. William Wheeler

1st Ohio Light Artillery,
Battery I (Six Napoleons)
Capt. Hubert Dilger

1st Ohio Light Artillery,
Battery K (Four Napoleons)
Capt. Lewis Heckman

4th United States Light Artillery,
Battery G (Six Napoleons)
Lt. Bayard Wilkeson (mw-c)
Lt. Eugene A. Bancroft

XII ARMY CORPS
Maj. Gen. Henry W. Slocum
Brig. Gen. Alpheus S. Williams

Headquarters Guard and Orderlies

9th New York Cavalry, Companies D and L
Capt. Joseph G. Weld

Provost Guard

10th Maine (3 companies)
Capt. John D. Beardsley

FIRST DIVISION
Brig. Gen. Alpheus S. Williams
Brig. Gen. Thomas H. Ruger

First Brigade
Col. Archibald L. McDougall

5th Connecticut
Col. Warren W. Packer

20th Connecticut
Lt. Col. William B. Wooster

3rd Maryland
Col. Joseph M. Sudsburg

123rd New York
Lt. Col. James C. Rogers

145th New York
Col. Edward L. Price

46th Pennsylvania
Col. James L. Selfridge

Second Brigade
Brig. Gen. Henry H. Lockwood

1st Maryland Potomac Home Brigade
Col. William P. Maulsby

1st Maryland Eastern Shore
Col. James Wallace

150th New York
Col. John H. Ketcham

Third Brigade
Brig. Gen. Thomas H. Ruger
Col. Silas Colgrove

27th Indiana
Col. Silas Colgrove
Lt. Col. John R. Fesler

2nd Massachusetts
Lt. Col. Charles R. Mudge (k)
Maj. Charles F. Morse

13th New Jersey
Col. Ezra A. Carman

107th New York
Col. Nirom M. Crane

3rd Wisconsin
Col. William Hawley

SECOND DIVISION
Brig. Gen. John W. Geary

Provost Guard

28th Pennsylvania, Company B
Lt. George W. Newmeyer

First Brigade
Col. Charles Candy

5th Ohio
Col. John H. Patrick

7th Ohio
Col. William R. Creighton

29th Ohio
Capt. Wilbur F. Stevens (w)
Capt. Edward Hayes

66th Ohio
Lt. Col. Eugene Powell

28th Pennsylvania (9 companies)
Capt. John H. Flynn

147th Pennsylvania (8 companies)
Lt. Col. Ario Pardee, Jr.

Second Brigade
Col. George A. Cobham, Jr.
(final command of regiment)
Brig. Gen. Thomas L. Kane

29th Pennsylvania
Col. William Rickards, Jr.

109th Pennsylvania
Capt. Frederick L. Gimber

111th Pennsylvania
Lt. Col. Thomas L. Walker
(final command of regiment)
Col. George A. Cobham, Jr.

Third Brigade
Brig. Gen. George S. Greene

60th New York
Col. Abel Godard

78th New York
Lt. Col. Herbert von Hammerstein

102nd New York
Col. James C. Lane (w)
Capt. Lewis R. Stegman

137th New York
Col. David Ireland

149th New York
Col. Henry A. Barnum
(final command of regiment)
Lt. Col. Charles B. Randall (w)
Capt. Nicholas Grumbach

Artillery Brigade
Lt. Edward D. Muhlenberg

1st New York Light Artillery,
Battery M (Four 10-pounder Parrotts)
Lt. Charles E. Winegar

Pennsylvania Light Artillery,
Battery E (Six 10-pounder Parrotts)
Lt. Charles A. Atwell

4th United States Light Artillery,
Battery F (Six Napoleons)
Lt. Sylvanus T. Rugg

5th United States Light Artillery,
Battery K (Four Napoleons)
Lt. David H. Kinzie

CAVALRY CORPS
Maj. Gen. Alfred Pleasonton

Provost Guard

6th United States Cavalry, Companies D and K
Lt. James F. Wade

FIRST DIVISION
Brig. Gen. John Buford

United States Signal Corps (detachment)
Lt. Aaron B. Jerome

First Brigade
Col. William Gamble

8th Illinois
Maj. John L. Beveridge

12th Illinois (4 companies) and
3rd Indiana (6 companies)
Col. George H. Chapman
(Capt. George W. Shears had subordinate
command of 12th Illinois)

8th New York
Lt. Col. William L. Markell

Artillery
2nd United States Horse Artillery,
Battery A (Six 3-inch Ordnance Rifles)
Lt. John H. Calef

Second Brigade
Col. Thomas C. Devin

Provost Guard
6th New York Cavalry, Company L
Capt. Harrison White

6th New York (6 companies)
Maj. William E. Beardsley

9th New York
Col. William Sackett

17th Pennsylvania
Col. Josiah H. Kellogg

3rd West Virginia (2 companies)
Capt. Seymour B. Conger

Reserve Brigade
Brig. Gen. Wesley Merritt

6th Pennsylvania Cavalry (10 companies)
Maj. James H. Haseltine

1st United States Cavalry
Capt. Richard S.C. Lord

2nd United States Cavalry
Capt. Theophilus F. Rodenbough

5th United States Cavalry
Capt. Julius W. Mason

Artillery
1st United States Horse Artillery,
Battery K (Six 3-inch Ordnance Rifles)
Capt. William M. Graham
(Attached July 3 only)

6th United States Cavalry (not on battlefield;
engagement at Fairfield, July 3)
Maj. Samuel H. Starr (w-c)
Capt. George C. Cram (c)
Lt. Louis H. Carpenter (final command of regiment)
Lt. Nicholas Nolan

SECOND DIVISION
Brig. Gen. David McM. Gregg

First Brigade
Col. John B. McIntosh

1st Maryland Cavalry (11 companies)
Lt. Col. James M. Deems

Purnell (Maryland) Legion, Company A
Capt. Robert E. Duvall

1st New Jersey Cavalry (9 companies)
Maj. M. H. Beaumont

1st Pennsylvania Cavalry
Col. John P. Taylor

3rd Pennsylvania Cavalry
Lt. Col. Edward S. Jones

Artillery

3rd Pennsylvania Heavy Artillery,
Battery H (One Section)
(Two 3-inch Ordnance Rifles)
Capt. William D. Rank

Second Brigade
(Not on battlefield;
at Westminster, MD guarding trains)
Col. Pennock Huey

2nd New York Cavalry
Lt. Col. Otto Harhaus

4th New York Cavalry
Lt. Col. Augustus Pruyn

6th Ohio Cavalry
Maj. William Stedman

8th Pennsylvania Cavalry
Capt. William A. Corrie

Artillery

3rd United States Horse Artillery
(Six 3-inch Ordnance Rifles)
Lt. William D. Fuller

Third Brigade
Col. J. Irvin Gregg

1st Maine Cavalry
Lt. Col. Charles H. Smith

10th New York Cavalry
Maj. M. Henry Avery

4th Pennsylvania Cavalry
Lt. Col. William E. Doster

16th Pennsylvania Cavalry
Lt. Col. John K. Robison

133

THIRD DIVISION
Brig. Gen. H. Judson Kilpatrick

Headquarters Guards and Orderlies

1st Ohio Cavalry, Company A
Capt. Noah Jones

1st Ohio Cavalry, Company C
Capt. Samuel N. Stanford

First Brigade
Brig. Gen. Elon J. Farnsworth (k)
Col. Nathaniel P. Richmond

5th New York Cavalry
Maj. John Hammond

18th Pennsylvania Cavalry
Lt. Col. William P. Brinton

1st Vermont Cavalry
Lt. Col. Addison W. Preston

1st (West) Virginia Cavalry
Col. Nathaniel P. Richmond
Maj. Charles E. Capehart

Artillery
4th United States Horse Artillery,
Battery E (Four 3-inch Ordnance Rifles)
Lt. Samuel S. Elder

Second Brigade
Brig. Gen. George A. Custer

1st Michigan Cavalry
Col. Charles H. Town

5th Michigan Cavalry
Col. Russell A. Alger

6th Michigan Cavalry
Col. George Gray

7th Michigan Cavalry
Col. William D. Mann

Artillery
2nd United States Horse Artillery,
Battery M (Six 3-inch Ordnance Rifles)
Lt. Alexander C. M. Pennington, Jr.

1st United States Horse Artillery,
Batteries E and G (Four Napoleons)
(Attached July 3 only)
Capt. Alanson Randol

HORSE ARTILLERY

First Horse Artillery Brigade
Capt. James M. Robertson

(Batteries not otherwise attached, in reserve on field)
9th Michigan Horse Battery (Six 3-inch Ordnance Rifles)
Capt. Jabez J. Daniels

6th Independent New York Horse Artillery
(Six 3-inch Ordnance Rifles)
Capt. Joseph W. Martin

2nd United States Horse Artillery,
Batteries B and L (Six 3-inch Ordnance Rifles)
Lt. Edward Heaton

Second Horse Artillery Brigade
Capt. John C. Tidball
(All batteries attached to cavalry units)

ARTILLERY RESERVE
Brig. Gen. Robert O. Tyler
(Injured during fall from horse on July 3)
Capt. James M. Robertson

Headquarters Guard

32nd Massachusetts Infantry, Company C
Capt. Josiah C. Fuller

Trains Guard

4th New Jersey Infantry (7 companies)
Maj. Charles Ewing

First Regular Brigade
Capt. Dunbar R. Ransom (w)
1st United States Light Artillery,
Battery H (Six Napoleons)
Lt. Chandler P. Eakin (w)
Lt. Philip D. Mason
3rd United States Light Artillery,
Batteries F and K (Six Napoleons)
Lt. John G. Turnbull
4th United States Light Artillery,
Battery C (Six Napoleons)
Lt. Evan Thomas
5th United States Light Artillery,
Battery C (Six Napoleons)
Lt. Gulian V. Weir

First Volunteer Brigade
Lieut. Col. Freeman McGilvery
5th Massachusetts Light Artillery,
Battery E (Six 3-inch Ordnance Rifle)
Capt. Charles A. Phillips
9th Massachusetts Light Artillery,
(Six Napoleons)
Capt. John Bigelow (w)
Lt. Richard S. Milton
15th New York Independent Light Battery
(Four Napoleons)
Capt. Patrick Hart (w)
1st Pennsylvania Light Artillery,
Batteries C and F
(Six 3-inch Ordnance Rifles)
Capt. James Thompson

Second Volunteer Brigade
Capt. Elijah D. Taft
1st Connecticut Heavy Artillery,
Battery B (Four 4.5-inch Rifles)
(Not on the field – at Westminster, MD)
Capt. Albert F. Brooker
1st Connecticut Heavy Artillery,
Battery M (Four 4.5-inch Rifles)
(Not on the field – at Westminster, MD)
Capt. Franklin A. Pratt

2nd Connecticut Light Artillery
(Four 14-pounder James Rifles,
Two 12-pounder Howitzers)
Capt. John W. Sterling
5th New York Independent Light Battery
(Six 20-pounder Parrotts)
Capt. Elijah D. Taft

Third Volunteer Brigade
Capt. James F. Huntington
1st New Hampshire Light Artillery,
Battery A (Four 3-inch Ordnance Rifles)
Capt. Frederick M. Edgell
1st Ohio Light Artillery,
Battery H (Six 3-inch Ordnance Rifles)
Lt. George W. Norton
1st Pennsylvania Light Artillery,
Batteries F and G
(Six 3-inch Ordnance Rifles)
Capt. R. Bruce Ricketts
1st West Virginia Light Artillery,
Battery C (Four 10-pounder Parrotts)
Capt. Wallace Hill

Fourth Volunteer Brigade
Capt. Robert H. Fitzhugh
6th Maine Light Artillery,
Battery F (Four Napoleons)
Lt. Edwin B. Dow
1st Maryland Light Artillery,
Battery A (Six 3-inch Ordnance Rifles)
Capt. James H. Rigby
1st New Jersey Light Artillery,
Battery A (Six 10-pounder Parrotts)
Lt. Augustin N. Parsons
1st New York Light Artillery,
Battery G (Six Napoleons)
Capt. Nelson Ames
1st New York Light Artiller,
Battery K (Six 3-inch Ordnance Rifles)
Capt. Robert H. Fitzhugh

CONFEDERATE FORCES

ARMY OF NORTHERN VIRGINIA
Gen. Robert E. Lee, commanding

ARMY HEADQUARTERS
Col. Robert H. Chilton, Chief of Staff and Inspector General
Brig. Gen. William N. Pendleton, Chief of Artillery
Col. Armistead L. Long, Military Secretary and Acting Asst. Chief of Artillery
Lt. Col. Briscoe G. Baldwin, Chief of Ordnance
Lt. Col. Robert C. Cole, Chief of Commissary
Lt. Col. James L. Corely, Chief Quartermaster
Maj. Henry E. Young, Judge Advocate General
Maj. Walter H. Taylor, Aide-de-Camp and Assistant Adjutant General
Maj. Charles Marshall, Aide-de-Camp and Assistant Military Secretary
Maj. Charles Venable, Aide-de-Camp and Assistant Inspector General
Capt. Samuel R. Johnston, Engineer

Escort and Couriers

39th Battalion Virginia Cavalry, Pifer's Company and Brown's Company
Maj. John H. Richardson (w)

Pifer's Company
Capt. Augusts P. Pifer

Brown's Company
Capt. Samuel B. Brown
(during the reorganization of the battalion in the fall of 1863, Pifer's Company became Company A, and Brown's Company became Company C)

LONGSTREET'S CORPS
Lt. Gen. James Longstreet

McLAWS' DIVISION
Maj. Gen. Lafayette McLaws

Kershaw's Brigade
Brig. Gen. Joseph B. Kershaw
2nd South Carolina
Col. John D. Kennedy (w)
Lt. Col. Franklin Gaillard

3rd South Carolina
Maj. Robert C. Maffett
Col. James D. Nance

3rd South Carolina Battalion
Lt. Col. William G. Rice

7th South Carolina
Col. D. Wyatt Aiken

8th South Carolina
Col. John W. Henagan

15th South Carolina
Col. William DeSaussure (mw)
Maj. William M. Gist

Semmes' Brigade
Brig. General Paul J. Semmes (mw)
Col. Goode Bryan

10th Georgia
Col. John B. Weems

50th Georgia
Col. William R. Manning

51st Georgia
Col. Edward Ball

53rd Georgia
Col. James P. Simms

Barksdale's Brigade
Brig. General William Barksdale (mw-c)
Col. Benjamin G. Humphreys

13th Mississippi
Col. James W. Carter (k)
Lt. Col. Kennon McElroy (w)
Maj. John M. Bradley (mw)
Lt. Absalom H. Farrar (w-c)

17th Mississippi
Col. William D. Holder (w)
Lt. Col. John C. Fiser (w)
Maj. Andrew J. Pulliam (w)
Maj. Richard E. Jones (k)
Capt. Gwen R. Cherry

18th Mississippi
Col. Thomas M. Griffin (w)
Lt. Col. William H. Luse (c)
Maj. George B. Gerald

21st Mississippi
Col. Benjamin G. Humphreys

Wofford's Brigade
Brig. General William T. Wofford

16th Georgia
Col. Goode Bryan

18th Georgia
Lt. Col. Solon Z. Ruff

24th Georgia
Col. Robert McMillan

Cobb's (Georgia) Legion
Lt. Col. Luther J. Glenn

Phillips' (Georgia) Legion
Lt. Col. Elihu S. Barclay, Jr.

3rd Georgia Battalion Sharpshooters
Lt. Col. Nathan L. Hutchins, Jr.

Cabell's Artillery Battalion
Col. Henry C. Cabell

Manly's Battery,
1st North Carolina Artillery, Battery A
(Two Napoleons, Two 3-inch Ordnance Rifles)
Capt. Basil C. Manly

Fraser's Battery, Pulaski (Georgia) Artillery
(Two 3-inch Ordnance Rifles,
Two 10-pounder Parrotts)
Capt. John C. Fraser (mw)
Lieut. William J. Furlong

McCarthy's Battery,
1st Richmond Howitzers (Two Napoleons,
Two 3-inch Ordnance Rifles)
Capt. Edward S. McCarthy (w)
Lt. Robert M. Anderson

Carlton's Battery, Troup County (Georgia)
Artillery (Two 12-pounder Howitzers,
Two 10-pounder Parrotts)
Capt. Henry H. Carlton (w)
Lt. Columbus W. Motes

PICKETT'S DIVISION
Brig. General George E. Pickett

Garnett's Brigade
Brig. Gen. Robert B. Garnett (k)
Maj. Charles S. Peyton

8th Virginia
Col. Eppa Hunton (w)
Lt. Col. Norbonne Berkeley (w-c)
Maj. Edmund Berkeley (w)
Lt. John Gray

18th Virginia
Lt. Col. Henry A. Carrington (w-c)
Capt. Henry T. Owen

19th Virginia
Col. Henry Gantt (w)
Lt. Col. John T. Ellis (mw)
Maj. Charles S. Peyton

28th Virginia
Col. Robert C. Allen (k)
Lt. Col. William Watts

56th Virginia
Col. William D. Stuart (mw)
Lt. Col. Philip P. Slaughter

Kemper's Brigade
Brig. Gen. James L. Kemper (w-c, rescued)
Col. Joseph Mayo, Jr.

1st Virginia
Col. Lewis B. Williams, Jr. (k)
Lt. Col. Frederick G. Skinner

3rd Virginia
Col. Joseph Mayo, Jr.
Lt. Col. Alexander D. Callcote (k)
Maj. William H. Pryor

7th Virginia
Col. Waller T. Patton (mw-c)
Lt. Col. Charles C. Flowerree

11th Virginia
Maj. Kirkwood Otey (w)
Capt. James R. Hutter (w-c)
Capt. John H. Smith

24th Virginia
Col. William R. Terry (w)
Maj. Joseph A. Hambrick (w)
Capt. William N. Bentley

Armistead's Brigade
Brig. General Lewis A. Armistead
Lt. Col. William White (w)
Maj. Joseph R. Cabell
Col. William R. Aylett (w) (final command of brigade)

9th Virginia
Maj. John C. Owens (mw)
Capt. James J. Phillips

14th Virginia
Col. James G. Hodges (k)
Lt. Col. William White (w)
(final command of regiment)
Maj. Robert H. Moore (mw)

38th Virginia
Col. Edward C. Edmonds (k)
Lt. Col. Powhatan B. Whittle (mw)
Maj. Joseph R. Cabell

53rd Virginia
Col. William R. Aylett (w)
Lt. Col Rawley Martin (mw-c)
Maj. John Timberlake (c)
Capt. Henry Edmunds

57th Virginia
Col. John B. Magruder (mw-c)
Lt. Col. Benjamin H. Wade (mw)
Maj. Clement R. Fontaine

Dearing's Artillery Battalion
Major James Dearing

Stribling's Battery,
Fauquier (Virginia) Artillery
(Four Napoleons, Two 20-pounder Parrotts)
Capt. Robert M. Stribling

Caskie's Battery,
Richmond "Hampden" (Virginia) Artillery
(Two Napoleons, One 10-pounder Parrott,
One 3-inch Ordnance Rifle)
Capt. William H. Caskie

Macon's Battery,
Richmond "Fayette" Artillery
(Two Napoleons, Two 10-pounder Parrotts)
Capt. Miles C. Macon

Blount's Battery,
Lynchburg (Virginia) Artillery
(Four Napoleons)
Capt. Joseph G. Blount

HOOD'S DIVISION
Maj. Gen. John B. Hood (w)
Brig. Gen. Evander M. Law

Law's Brigade
Brig. Gen. Evander M. Law
Col. James L. Sheffield

4th Alabama
Col. Lawrence H. Scruggs

15th Alabama
Col. William C. Oates
Capt. Blanton A. Hill

44th Alabama
Col. William F. Perry

47th Alabama
Lt. Col. Michael J. Bulger (w-c)
Maj. James M. Campbell

48th Alabama
Col. James L. Sheffield
Capt. Thomas J. Eubanks (w)
Lt. Col. William McT. Hardwick (w)
Maj. Columbus B. St. John (w)
Capt. Jeremiah Edwards (c)
Lt. Francis M. Burk
Lt. Reuben T. Ewing

Robertson's Brigade
Brig. Gen. Jerome B. Robertson (w)

3rd Arkansas
Col. Van H. Manning (w)
Lt. Col. Robert S. Taylor

1st Texas
Col. Phillip A. Work
Maj. Frederick S. Bass

4th Texas
Col. John C. G. Key (w)
Lt. Col. Benjamin F. Carter (mw)
Maj. John P. Bane

5th Texas
Col. Robert M. Powell (w-)
Lt. Col. King Bryan (w)
Maj. Jefferson C. Rogers

Anderson's Brigade
Brig. General George T. Anderson (w)
Lt. Col. William T. Luffman (w)
Col. William W. White

7th Georgia
Col. William W. White
Lt. Col. George H. Carmichal

8th Georgia
Col. John R. Towers (w)

9th Georgia
Lt. Col. John C. Mounger (k)
Maj. William M. Jones (w)
Capt. James M. D. King (w)
Capt. George Hillyer

11th Georgia
Col. Francis H. Little (w)
Lt. Col. William Luffman (w)
Maj. Henry D. McDaniel

59th Georgia
Col. Jack Brown (w)
Maj. Bolivar H. Gee (w)
Capt. Mastin G. Bass

Benning's Brigade
Brig. General Henry L. Benning

2nd Georgia
Lt. Col. William T. Harris (k)
Maj. William S. Shepherd

15th Georgia
Col. Dudley M. DuBose

17th Georgia
Col. Wesley C. Hodges

20th Georgia
Col. John A. Jones (k)
Lt. Col. James D. Waddell

Henry's Artillery Battalion
Major Mathis W. Henry

Latham's Battery, "Branch" (North Carolina) Artillery (Three Napoleons, One 12-pounder Howitzer, One 6-pounder gun)
Capt. Alexander C. Latham

Bachman's Battery, "German" Charleston (South Carolina) Artillery (Four Napoleons)
Capt. William K. Bachman

Garden's Battery, Palmetto (South Carolina) Light Artillery (Two Napoleons, Two 10-pounder Parrotts)
Capt. Hugh R. Garden

Reilly's Battery, Rowan (North Carolina) Artillery (Two Napoleons, Two 3-inch Ordnance Rifles, Two 10-pounder Parrotts)
Capt. James Reilly

ARTILLERY RESERVE
(Longstreet's Corps)
Col. James B. Walton

Alexander's Battalion
Col. E. Porter Alexander
Woolfolk's Battery, Ashland (Virginia) Artillery (Two Napoleons, Two 20-pounder Parrotts)
Capt. Pichegru Woolfolk, Jr. (w)
Lt. James Woolfolk
Jordan's Battery, Bedford (Virginia) Artillery (Four 3-inch Ordnance Rifles)
Capt. Tyler C. Jordan
Gilbert's Battery, Brooks (South Carolina) Artillery (Four 12-pounder Howitzers)
Lt. S. Capers Gilbert
Moody's Battery, Madison (Louisiana) Light Artillery (Four 24-pounder Howitzers)
Capt. George V. Moody
Parker's Battery, Virginia (Richmond) Battery (Three 3-inch Ordnance Rifles, Four 10-pounder Parrott)
Capt. William W. Parker

Taylor's Battery, Virginia (Bath) Artillery (Four Napoleons)
Capt. Osmond B. Taylor

Washington (Louisiana) Artillery Battalion
Maj. Benjamin F. Eshleman

1st Company (One Napoleon)
Capt. Charles W. Squires

2nd Company (Two Napoleons, One 12-pounder Howitzer)
Capt. John B. Richardson

3rd Company (Three Napoleons)
Capt. Merritt B. Miller

4th Company (Two Napoleons, One 12-pounder Howitzer)
Capt. Joseph Norcom (w)
Lt. Harry A. Battles

EWELL'S CORPS
Lt. Gen. Richard S. Ewell

Escort and Orderlies
39th Battalion Virginia Cavalry,
Randolph's Company
Capt. William F. Randolph

Provost Guard
1st North Carolina Battalion,
Companies A and B

EARLY'S DIVISION
Maj. Gen. Jubal A. Early

Escort

35th Battalion Virginia Cavalry (attached)
Lt. Col. Elijah V. White

17th Virginia Cavalry (attached)
Lt. Col. William H. French

Hays' Brigade
Brig. General Harry T. Hays

5th Louisiana
Maj. Alexander Hart (w)
Capt. Thomas H. Briscoe

6th Louisiana
Lt. Col. Joseph Hanlon

7th Louisiana
Col. Davidson B. Penn

8th Louisiana
Col. Trevanion D. Lewis (k)
Lt. Col. Alcibiades de Blanc (w)
Maj. German A. Lester

9th Louisiana
Col. Leroy A. Stafford

Smith's Brigade
Brig. Gen. William Smith

13th Virginia
Col. John S. Hoffman

49th Virginia
Lt. Col. J. Catlett Gibson

52nd Virginia
Lt. Col. James H. Skinner (w)
Maj. John D. Ross

Hoke's Brigade
Col. Issac E. Avery (mw)
Col. Archibald C. Godwin

6th North Carolina
Maj. Samuel McD. Tate

21st North Carolina
Col. William W. Kirkland

57th North Carolina
Col. Archibald C. Godwin
Lt. Col. Hamilton C. Jones

Gordon's Brigade
Brig. Gen. John B. Gordon

13th Georgia
Col. James M. Smith

26th Georgia
Col. Edmund N. Atkinson

31st Georgia
Col. Clement A. Evans

38th Georgia
Capt. William L. McLeod (k)
Lt. John Oglesby (k)
Lt. William F. Goodwin (k)

60th Georgia
Capt. Walter B. Jones

61st Georgia
Col. John H. Lamar

Jones' Artillery Battalion
Lt. Col. Hilary P. Jones

Carrington's Battery, Charlottesville (Virginia)
Artillery (Four Napoleons)
Capt. James McD. Carrington

Tanner's Battery, "Courtney"
(Virginia) Artillery (Four Napoleons)
Capt. William A. Tanner

Green's Battery, Louisiana Guard Artillery
(Two 3-inch Ordnance Rifles,
Two 10-pounder Parrotts)
Capt. Charles A. Green

Garber's Battery, Staunton (Virginia) Artillery
(Four Napoleons)
Capt. Asher W. Garber

RODES' DIVISION
Maj. General Robert E. Rodes

Daniel's Brigade
Brig. Gen. Junius Daniel

32nd North Carolina
Col. Edmund C. Brabble

43rd North Carolina
Col. Thomas S. Kenan (w-c)
Lt. Col. William G. Lewis

45th North Carolina
Lt. Col. Samuel H. Boyd (w-c)
Maj. John R. Winston (w-c)
Capt. Alexander H. Gallaway (w)
Capt. James A. Hopkins

53rd North Carolina
Col. William A. Owens

2nd North Carolina Battalion
Lt. Col. Hezekiah L. Andrews (k)
Maj. John M. Hancock (w-c)
Capt. Van Brown

Iverson's Brigade
Brig. Gen. Alfred Iverson

5th North Carolina
Capt. Speight B. West (w)
Capt. Benjamin Robinson (w)

12th North Carolina
Lt. Col. William S. Davis

20th North Carolina
Lt. Col. Nelson Slough (w)
Maj. John S. Brooks (w)
Capt. Lewis T. Hicks

23rd North Carolina
Col. Daniel H. Christie (mw)
Maj. Charles C. Blacknall (w-c)
Capt. Abner D. Peace (w)
Capt. William H. Johnston (w)
Capt. Vines E. Turner

Doles' Brigade
Brig. General George Doles

4th Georgia
Lt. Col. David R. E. Winn (k)
Maj. William H. Willis

12th Georgia
Col. Edward Willis

21st Georgia
Col. John T. Mercer

44th Georgia
Col. Samuel P. Lumpkin (w-c)
Maj. William H. Peebles

Ramseur's Brigade
Brig. Gen. Stephen D. Ramseur

2nd North Carolina
Maj. Daniel W. Hurtt (w)
Capt. James T. Scales

4th North Carolina
Col. Bryan Grimes

14th North Carolina
Col. R. Tyler Bennett (w)
Maj. Joseph H. Lambeth

30th North Carolina
Col. Francis M. Parker (w)
Maj. William W. Sillers

O'Neal's Brigade
Colonel Edward A. O'Neal

3rd Alabama
Col. Cullen A. Battle

5th Alabama
Col. Josephus M. Hall

6th Alabama
Col. James N. Lightfoot (w)
Capt. Milledge L. Bowie

12th Alabama
Col. Samuel B. Pickens

26th Alabama
Lt. Col. John C. Goodgame

141

Carter's Artillery Battalion
Lt. Col. Thomas H. Carter

Reese's Battery, Jeff Davis (Alabama) Artillery (Four 3-inch Ordnance Rifles)
Capt. William J. Reese

Carter's Battery,
King William (Virginia) Artillery
(Two Napoleons, Two 10-pounder Parrotts)
Capt. William P. Carter

Page's Battery,
Lousia "Morris" (Virginia) Artillery
(Four Napoleons)
Capt. Richard C. M. Page (w)
Lt. Samuel H. Pendleton

Fry's Battery,
Richmond "Orange" (Virginia) Artillery
(Two 3-inch Ordnance Rifles,
Two 10-pounder Parrotts)
Capt. Charles W. Fry

JOHNSON'S DIVISION
Maj. Gen. Edward Johnson

Steuart's Brigade
Brig. Gen. George H. Steuart

1st Maryland Battalion
Lt. Col. James R. Herbert (w)
Maj. William W. Goldsborough (w-c)
Capt. James P. Crane

1st North Carolina
Lt. Col. Hamilton A. Brown

3rd North Carolina
Maj. Willliam M. Parsley

10th Virginia
Capt. William B. Yancey

23rd Virginia
Lt. Col. Simeon T. Walton

37th Virginia
Maj. Henry C. Wood

Nicholls' Brigade
Col. Jesse M. Williams

1st Louisiana
Col. Michael Nolan (k)
Capt. Edward D. Willett

2nd Louisiana
Lt. Col. Ross E. Burke (w-c)

10th Louisiana
Maj. Thomas N. Powell

14th Louisiana
Lt. Col. David Zable

15th Louisiana
Maj. Andrew Brady

Stonewall Brigade
Brig. General James Walker

2nd Virginia
Col. John Q. A. Nadenbousch

4th Virginia
Maj. William Terry

5th Virginia
Col. John H. S. Funk

27th Virginia
Lt. Col. Daniel M. Shriver

33rd Virginia
Col. Jacob B. Golladay

Jones' Brigade
Brig. Gen. John M. Jones (w)
Lt. Col. Robert H. Dungan

21st Virginia
Capt. William P. Moseley

25th Virginia
Col. John C. Higginbotham (w)
Lt. Col. John A. Robinson

42nd Virginia
Col. Robert Withers (w)
Capt. Samuel H. Saunders

44th Virginia
Maj. Norval Cobb (w)
Capt. Thomas R. Buckner

48th Virginia
Lt. Col. Robert H. Dungan
Maj. Oscar White

50th Virginia
Lt. Col. Logan H. N. Salyer

Latimer's Artillery Battalion
Maj. James W. Latimer (mw)
Capt. Charles I. Raine

Dement's Battery,
1st Maryland Battery
(Four Napoleons)
Capt. William F. Dement

Carpenter's Battery,
Alleghany Rough (Virginia) Artillery
(Two Napoleons, Two 3-inch Ordnance Rifles)
Capt. John C. Carpenter

Brown's Battery,
4th Maryland Chesapeake Artillery
(Four 10-pounder Parrotts)
Capt. William D. Brown (mw)

Raine's Battery,
Lynchburg (Virginia) "Lee" Battery
(One 3-inch Ordnance Rifle,
One 10-pounder Parrott,
Two 20-pounder Parrotts)
Capt. Charles I. Raine
Lt. William M. Hardwicke

ARTILLERY RESERVE
Colonel J. Thompson Brown, Chief of Artillery

Dance's Artillery Battalion, 1st Virginia Artillery
Capt. Willis J. Dance

Watson's Battery,
2nd Richmond (Virginia) Howitzers
(Four 10-pounder Parrotts)
Capt. David Watson

Smith's Battery,
3rd Richmond (Virginia) Howitzers
(Four 3-inch Ordnance Rifles)
Capt. Benjamin H. Smith, Jr.

Cunningham's Battery,
Powhatan (Virginia) Artillery
(Four 3-inch Ordnance Rifles)
Lt. John M. Cunningham

Graham's Battery,
1st Rockbridge (Virginia) Artillery
(Four 20-pounder Parrotts)
Capt. Archibald Graham

Griffin's (Hupp's) Salem (Virginia)
Flying Artillery
(Two Napoleons, Two 3-inch
Ordnance Rifles)
Lt. Charles B. Griffin

Nelson's Battalion
Lt. Colonel William Nelson

Amherst (Virginia) Artillery
(Three Napoleons,
One 3-inch Ordnance Rifle)
Capt. Thomas J. Kirkpatrick

Fluvanna (Virginia) Artillery
(Three Napoleons,
One 3-inch Ordnance Rifle)
Capt. John L. Massie

Georgia Battery
(Two 3-inch Ordnance Rifles,
One 10-pounder Parrott)
Capt. John Milledge, Jr.

HILL'S CORPS
Lt. Gen. Ambrose P. Hill

ANDERSON'S DIVISION
Maj. General Richard H. Anderson

Wilcox's Brigade
Brig. Gen. Cadmus M. Wilcox

8th Alabama
Lt. Col. Hilary A. Herbert

9th Alabama
Capt. J. Horace King (w)
Capt. John N. Chisholm (w-c)
Capt. Gaines C. Smith (w-c)
Capt. M G. May (w)

10th Alabama
Col. William H. Forney (w-c)
Lt. Col. James E. Shelley

11th Alabama
Col. John C. C. Sanders (w)
Lt. Col. George E. Tayloe

14th Alabama
Col. Lucius Pinckard (w-c)
Lt. Col. James A. Broome

Wright's Brigade
Brig. Gen. Ambrose R. Wright
(final command of brigade)
Col. William Gibson (w-c)

3rd Georgia
Col. Edward J. Walker

22nd Georgia
Col. Joseph A. Wasden (k)
Capt. Benjamin C. McCurry

48th Georgia
Col. William Gibson (w-c)
Capt. Matthew R. Hall

2nd Georgia Battalion
Maj. George W. Ross (mw-c)
Capt. Charles J. Moffett

Mahone's Brigade
Brig. Gen. William Mahone

6th Virginia
Col. George T. Rogers

12th Virginia
Col. David A. Weisiger

16th Virginia
Col. Joseph H. Ham

41st Virginia
Col. William A. Parham

61st Virginia
Col. Virginius D. Groner

Perry's Brigade
Col. David Lang

2nd Florida
Maj. Walter R. Moore (w-c)
Capt. William D. Ballantine (w-c)
Capt. C. Seton Fleming

5th Florida
Capt. Richmond N. Gardner (w)
Capt. J. S. Cochran (mw)
Capt. Council A. Bryan
Capt. John W. Hollyman

8th Florida
Lt. Col. William Baya

Posey's Brigade
Brig. Gen. Carnot Posey

12th Mississippi
Col. William H. Taylor

16th Mississippi
Col. Samuel E. Baker

19th Mississippi
Col. Nathaniel H. Harris

48th Mississippi
Col. Joseph M. Jayne

11th Georgia "Sumter" Artillery Battalion
Maj. John Lane

Company A
(One 12-pounder Howitzer,
One Napoleon, One 3-inch Navy Rifle,
Three 10-pounder Parrotts)
Capt. Hugh M. Ross

Company B
(Four 12-pounder Howitzers,
Two Napoleons)
Capt. George M. Patterson

Company C
(Three 3-inch Navy Rifles,
Two 10-pounder Parrotts)
Capt. John T. Wingfield (w)

HETH'S DIVISION
Maj. Gen. Henry Heth (w)
Brig. Gen. J. Johnston Pettigrew (w)

Pettigrew's Brigade
Brig. General James J. Pettigrew (w)
Col. James K. Marshall (w)
Maj. John T. Jones (w)

11th North Carolina
Col. Collett Leventhorpe (w-c)
Maj. Egbert A. Ross (k)
Capt. Francis W. Bird

26th North Carolina
Col. Henry K. Burgwyn, Jr. (k)
Lt. Col. John R. Lane (w)
Maj. John T. Jones
Capt. Henry C. Albright

47th North Carolina
Col. George H. Faribault (w)
Lt. Col. John A. Graves (mw-c)
Lt. Col. J. Owens Rogers

52nd North Carolina
Col. James K. Marshall (k)
Lt. Col. Marcus A. Parks (w-c)
Maj. John Q. Richardson (mw-c)
Capt. Nathaniel A. Foster

Brockenbrough's Brigade
Col. John M. Brockenborough

40th Virginia
Capt. T. Edwin Betts
Capt. R. B. Davis

47th Virginia
Col. Robert M. Mayo
Lt. Col. John W. Lyell

55th Virginia
Col. William S. Christian

22nd Virginia Battalion
Maj. John S. Bowles

Archer's Brigade
Brig. Gen. James J. Archer (c)
Col. Birkett D. Fry (w-c)
Lt. Col. Samuel G. Shepard

5th Alabama Battalion
Maj. Albert S. Van De Graaf

13th Alabama
Col. Birkett D. Fry (w-c)
Capt. Charles F. Chambers (w-c)
Capt. N. J. Taylor

1st Tennessee (Provisional Army)
Lt. Col. Newton J. George (c)
Maj. Felix G. Buchanan (w)
Capt. Jacob B Turney

7th Tennessee
Col. John A. Fite (c)
Lt. Col. Samuel G. Shepard

14th Tennessee
Capt. Bruce L. Phillips

Davis' Brigade
Brig. Gen. Joseph R. Davis

2nd Mississippi
Col. John M. Stone (w)
Maj. John A. Blair (c)
Lt. Col. David W. Humphries (k)

11th Mississippi
Col. Francis M. Green (w)
Maj. Reuben D. Reynolds (w)
Lt. Daniel Featherston (k)
Lt. Robert A. McDowell

42nd Mississippi
Col. Hugh R. Miller (mw-c)
Lt. Col. Hillary Moseley (w)
Maj. William A. Feeney (w)
Capt. Andrew M. Nelson

55th North Carolina
Col. John K. Connally (w-c)
Lt. Col. Maurice T. Smith (mw)
Maj. Alfred H. Belo (w)
Capt. George A. Gilreath (k)
Capt. E. Fletcher Satterfield

Garnett's Artillery Battalion
Lt. Col. John Garnett

Maurin's Battery,
Donaldsville (Louisiana) Artillery
(Two 3-inch Ordnance Rifles,
One 10-pounder Parrott)
Capt. Victor Maurin

Moore's Battery,
Huger (Virginia) Artillery
(Two Napoleons, One 3-inch Ordnance Rifle,
One 10-pounder Parrott)
Capt. Joseph D. Moore

Lewis' Battery,
Pittsylvania (Virginia) Artillery
(Two Napoleons, Two 3-inch Ordnance Rifles)
Capt. John W. Lewis

Grandy's Battery,
Norfolk (Virginia) Light Artillery Blues
(Two 3-inch Ordnance Rifles,
Two 12-pounder Howitzers)
Capt. Charles R. Grandy

PENDER'S DIVISION
Maj. Gen. Willian D. Pender (mw)
Brig. Gen. James H. Lane
(final command of division)
Maj. Gen. Isaac R. Trimble (w-c)

Perrin's Brigade
Col. Abner Perrin

1st South Carolina (Provisional Army)
Maj. Charles W. McCreary

1st South Carolina Rifles
Capt. William M. Hadden

12th South Carolina
Col. John L. Miller

13th South Carolina
Lt. Col. Benjamin T. Brockman

14th South Carolina
Lt. Col. Joseph N. Brown (w)
Maj. Edward Croft (w)
Capt. James Boatwright

Lane's Brigade
Brig. Gen. James H. Lane
Col. Clark M. Avery

7th North Carolina
Capt. J. Mcleod Turner (w-c)
Capt. James G. Harris

18th North Carolina
Col. John D. Barry

28th North Carolina
Col. Samuel D. Lowe (w)
Lt. Col. William H. A. Speer

33rd North Carolina
Col. Clark M. Avery
Maj. Joseph H. Saunders (w-c)
Lt. Wesley L. Battle (mw)
Lt. W. C. Horton (w)

37th North Carolina
Col. William M. Barbour

Thomas' Brigade
Brig. Gen. Edward L. Thomas

14th Georgia
Col. Robert W. Folsom

35th Georgia
Col. Bolling H. Holt

45th Georgia
Col. Thomas J. Simmons

49th Georgia
Col. Samuel T. Player

Scales' Brigade
Brig. Gen. Alfred M. Scales (w)
Lt. Col. George T. Gordon (w)
Col. W. Lee J. Lowrance

13th North Carolina
Col. Joseph H. Hyman (w)
Lt. Col. Henry A. Rogers

16th North Carolina
Capt. Leroy W. Stowe
Capt. Abel S. Cloud

22nd North Carolina
Col. James Conner

34th North Carolina
Col. W. Lee J. Lowrance
Lt. Col. George T. Gordon (w)
Lt. Alexander A. Cathey (w-c)
Lt. Burwell T. Cotton

38th North Carolina
Col. William J. Hoke (w)
Lt. Col. John Ashford (w)
Capt. William L. Thornburg (w)
Lt. John M. Robinson

Poague's Artillery Battalion
Maj. William T. Poague

Wyatt's Battery,
Albemarle (Virginia) Artillery
(Two 3-inch Ordnance Rifles,
One 10-pounder Parrotts,
One 12-pounder Howitzer)
Capt. James W. Wyatt

Graham's Battery,
Charlotte (North Carolina) Artillery
(Two Napoleons, Two 12-pounder Howitzers)
Capt. Joseph Graham

Ward's Battery,
Madison (Mississippi) Light Artillery
(Three Napoleons, One 12-pounder Howitzer)
Capt. George Ward

Brooke's Battery,
Virginia (Warrington) Battery
(Two Napoleons, Two 12-pounder Howitzers)
Capt. James V. Brooke

ARTILLERY RESERVE (HILL'S CORPS)
Col. R. Lindsay Walker
McIntosh's Battalion
Major David G. McIntosh

Rice's Battery,
Danville (Virginia) Artillery
(Four Napoleons)
Capt. R. Sidney Rice

Hurt's Battery, Hardaway (Alabama)
Artillery (Two 3-inch Ordnance Rifles,
Two Whitworth Rifles)
Capt. William B. Hurt

Wallace's Battery, 2nd Rockbridge (Virginia)
Artillery (Four 3-inch Ordnance Rifles)
Lt. Samuel Wallace

Johnson's Battery, Richmond (Virginia)
Battery (Two Napoleons,
Two 3-inch Ordnance Rifles)
Capt. Marmaduke Johnson

Pegram's Artillery Battalion
Maj. William R. J. Pegram

Crenshaw's Battery,
Richmond (Virginia) Battery
(Two Napoleons, Two 12-pounder Howitzers)
Capt. William G. Crenshaw

Marye's Battery,
Fredericksburg (Virginia) Artillery
(Two Napoleons, Two 10-pounder Parrotts)
Capt. Edward A. Marye

Brander's Battery,
"Letcher" Richmond (Virginia) Artillery
(Two Napoleons, Two 10-pounder Parrotts)
Capt. Thomas A. Brander

Zimmerman's Battery,
Pee Dee (South Carolina) Artillery
(Four 3-inch Ordnance Rifles)
Capt. Ervin B. Brunson
Lt. William E. Zimmerman

McGraw's Battery,
"Purcell" (Virginia) Artillery
(Four Napoleons)
Capt. Joseph McGraw

CAVALRY DIVISION
Maj. Gen. James Ewell Brown Stuart

Hampton's Brigade
Brig. Gen. Wade Hampton (w)
Col. Laurence S. Baker

1st North Carolina Cavalry
Col. Laurence S. Baker
Lt. Col. James B. Gordon

1st South Carolina Cavalry
Lt. Col. John D. Twiggs
*(Col. John L. Black, wounded at Upperville,
later stated that Maj. William Walker
commanded the regiment at this time)*

2nd South Carolina Cavalry
Maj. Thomas J. Lipscomb

Cobb's (Georgia) Legion
Col. Pierce M. B. Young

Jeff Davis (Mississippi) Legion
Col. Joseph F. Waring

Phillips' (Georgia) Legion
Lt. Col. Elihu S. Barclay, Jr.

Fitz Lee's Brigade
Brig. Gen. W. Fitzhugh Lee

1st Virginia Cavalry
Col. James H. Drake

2nd Virginia Cavalry
Col. Thomas T. Munford

3rd Virginia Cavalry
Col. Thomas H. Owen

4th Virginia Cavalry
Col. Williams C. Wickham

5th Virginia Cavalry
Col. Thomas L. Rosser

1st Maryland Battalion
Maj. Harry Gilmor
Maj. Ridgely Brown
*(From July 2-4, Gilmore was provost marshal in the
town of Gettysburg)*

W. H. F. Lee's Brigade
Colonel John R. Chambliss, Jr.
(final command of brigade)
Col. J. Lucius Davis

2nd North Carolina Cavalry
Capt. William A. Graham, Jr. (w)
Lt. Joseph Baker

9th Virginia Cavalry
Col. Richard L. T. Beale

10th Virginia Cavalry
Col. J. Lucius Davis

13th Virginia Cavalry
Capt. Benjamin F. Winfield

Jenkins' Brigade
Brig. Gen. Albert G. Jenkins (w)
Colonel Milton J. Ferguson
Lt. Col. Vincent A. Witcher
(Ferguson was detailed to guard
prisoners in the town on July 3)

14th Virginia Cavalry
Maj. Benjamin F. Eakle

16th Virginia Cavalry
Col. Milton J. Ferguson
Maj. James H. Nounnan

17th Virginia Cavalry
Col. William H. French

34th Battalion Virginia Cavalry
Lt. Col. Vincent A. Witcher

36th Battalion Virginia Cavalry
Capt. Cornelius T. Smith

Artillery
Jackson's (Virginia) Battery
Charlottesville Horse Artillery
(Two 3-inch Ordnance Rifles
Two 12-pounder Howitzers)
Capt. Thomas E. Jackson

Stuart Horse Artillery
Maj. Robert F. Beckham

Breathed's (Virginia) Battery,
1st Stuart Horse Artillery
(Four 3-inch Ordnance Rifles)
Capt. James Breathed

Chew's (Virginia) Battery,
Ashby Horse Artillery
(One 3-inch Ordnance Rifle,
One 12-pounder Howizer)
Capt. R. Preston Chew

Griffin's (Maryland) Battery,
2nd Baltimore Battery
(Four 10-pounder Parrotts)
Capt. William H. Griffin

Hart's (South Carolina) Battery, Washington
Horse Artillery (Three Blakely Rifles)
Capt. James F. Hart

McGregor's (Virginia) Battery,
2nd Stuart Horse Artillery
(One Blakely Rifle, One unknown)
Capt. William M. McGregor

Units not engaged on the main
battlefield, July 1-3
Jones' Brigade
(Engaged at Fairfield, PA on July 3)
Brig. Gen. William E. Jones

6th Virginia Cavalry
Maj. Cabell E. Flournoy

7th Virginia Cavalry
Lt. Col. Thomas Marshall

11th Virginia Cavalry
Col. Lunsford L. Lomax

Imboden's Northwestern Brigade
Brig. Gen. John D. Imboden

18th Virginia Cavalry
Col. George W. Imboden

62nd Virginia Mounted Infantry
Col. George H. Smith

Virginia Partisan Rangers
Capt. John H. McNeill

Artillery
McClanahan's Battery,
Staunton (Virginia) Horse Artillery
(Six unknown guns)
Capt. John H. McClanahan

Robertson's Brigade
Brig. Gen. Beverly H. Robertson

4th North Carolina Cavalry
Col. Dennis D. Ferebee

5th North Carolina Cavalry
Lt. Col. Stephen B. Evans
Lt. Col. James A. Broome

The Gettysburg Address

The thousands of dead from both sides were eventually buried in shallow graves scattered across the battlefield. Individual resting places dotted fields, yards, and gardens, and mass burial trenches containing large numbers of bodies were prepared where the heaviest fighting took place. Several prominent Gettysburg citizens pursued plans to establish a suitable cemetery for the Union dead. Attorney David Wills urged Pennsylvania Governor Andrew G. Curtin to purchase land for a National Cemetery. Eventually, 17 acres adjoining the town's Evergreen Cemetery were secured for the new burial ground.

Dedicatory ceremonies for the new cemetery were set for Thursday, November 19, 1863. Wills invited a famous orator named Edward Everett to deliver the keynote speech. Wills also invited President Abraham Lincoln to attend and formally "set apart these grounds to their sacred use by a few appropriate remarks." Lincoln arrived in Gettysburg by train on November 18. He spent that night in Wills' home (which still stands on the town square), and likely added some finishing touches to his speech there.

The ceremonies began early the following afternoon in front of an estimated crowd of 15,000 that included recuperating Federal soldiers wounded during the battle. After Everett's two-hour oration and a hymn, Lincoln rose to deliver his short speech. When he finished, a moment of silence ensued followed by what one eyewit-

ness described as "barely polite" applause. Lincoln himself wondered whether his speech was a failure.

"The Gettysburg Address" was so short many in the crowd missed it, but the words and meaning still echo through history. In just a few words Lincoln framed the war as a necessary pain in the nation's "new birth of freedom," and confirmed that the ideals set forth at the formation of the country would live on through the sacrifice and victory of the Union soldiers.

Lincoln delivered to the country and to the world the most poignant, concise, and effective speech ever delivered.

Abraham Lincoln's GETTYSBURG ADDRESS

Four score and seven years ago our fathers brought forth on this continent, a new nation, conceived in Liberty, and dedicated to the proposition that all men are created equal.

Now we are engaged in a great civil war, testing whether that nation or any nation so conceived and so dedicated, can long endure. We are met on a great battle-field of that war. We have come to dedicate a portion of that field, as a final resting place for those who here gave their lives that that nation might live. It is altogether fitting and proper that we should do this.

But, in a larger sense, we can not dedicate — we can not consecrate — we can not hallow — this ground. The brave men, living and dead, who struggled here, have consecrated it, far above our poor power to add or detract. The world will little note, nor long remember what we say here, but it can never forget what they did here. It is for us the living, rather, to be dedicated here to the unfinished work which they who fought here have thus far so nobly advanced. It is rather for us to be here dedicated to the great task remaining before us — that from these honored dead we take increased devotion to that cause for which they gave the last full measure of devotion — that we here highly resolve that these dead shall not have died in vain — that this nation, under God, shall have a new birth of freedom — and that government of the people, by the people, for the people, shall not perish from the earth.

November 19. 1863.   Abraham Lincoln.

Gettysburg Personalities

This section includes biographical accounts of select Union and Confederate officers and soldiers who served at Gettysburg, as well as Gettysburg civilians and battlefield photographers.

The army commanders, Gens. George G. Meade and Robert E. Lee, are included together with entries for several of their corps commanders, additional officers, and a few others whose actions deserve note. Everyone who served at Gettysburg had a unique story. Hopefully this small sampling will motivate you to search out more information on these and other men whose lives were altered – and in some cases ended – in Pennsylvania during the summer of 1863.

Union Officers and Soldiers

Maj. Gen. George Gordon Meade
Commander, Army of the Potomac
(December 31, 1815 – November 6, 1872)

The pinnacle of George Meade's military career arrived in early July 1863 when he defeated Robert E. Lee' Army of Northern Virginia at Gettysburg.

When Maj. Gen. Joseph Hooker, commander of the Army of the Potomac, resigned on June 28, 1863, Lincoln selected Meade to replace him. The Pennsylvania Campaign was already well underway. The main battle began on July 1. Meade skillfully deployed his forces on commanding high ground south and southeast of the town and remained in place to defeat Lee on both July 2 and 3. On July 4 the Southerners began retreating from the field.

Although criticized in many circles for not conducting a more aggressive pursuit after the battle, Meade retained command of the Army of the Potomac for the rest of the war, serving under overall Federal commander Lt. Gen. Ulysses S. Grant. After the war Meade held various military commands and served as commissioner of Fairmount Park in Philadelphia until his death from pneumonia. He is buried in Philadelphia's Laurel Hill Cemetery.

Maj. Gen. John Fulton Reynolds

Commander, I Corps
(September 20, 1820 – July 1, 1863)

(LIBRARY OF CONGRESS)

The officer who committed Federal infantry into the fighting on the morning of the first day at Gettysburg, Reynolds was the highest-ranking officer on either side to be killed there.

He was the leader of the I Corps—and in command of the army's Left Wing, which included operational control over three corps—when the Battle of Gettysburg began on the morning of July 1. His was the first Federal infantry to arrive on the field, relieving Brig. Gen. John Buford's Federal cavalry who had been resisting the Confederate advance west of town. Reynolds was personally directing the placement of an infantry regiment along McPherson's Ridge when he was shot in the back of the head and knocked from his saddle. He died within minutes and was taken home to his native Lancaster, where he was buried on July 4.

Reynolds' decision to support Buford on July 1 and continue defending the ground at Gettysburg escalated what was at that point a meeting engagement into a major pitched battle that some argue forever after altered the course of the Civil War.

Maj. Gen. Winfield Scott Hancock

Commander, II Corps
(February 14, 1824 – February 9, 1886)

(LIBRARY OF CONGRESS)

Winfield S. Hancock might best be described by a staff officer's observation that "One felt safe when near him." It was Hancock's corps that bore the brunt of Pickett's Charge at Gettysburg on July 3.

Hancock arrived on the field at Gettysburg on the afternoon of the first day of fighting. Although he was not the senior Federal officer on the field, he was given tactical command by army commander Maj. Gen. George G. Meade. Hancock assisted other officers in establishing and strengthening a concave Federal defensive position along Cemetery Hill and Cemetery Ridge south and southeast of town.

On July 3, the Southern infantry assault known as Pickett's Charge was aimed squarely against Hancock's troops. He was close to the action directing his men from horseback when he was shot in the upper thigh, but refused to leave the field until the assault was repulsed. Although he never fully recovered, he did return to the field in the spring of 1864 to command his corps in the 1864 Overland Campaign. The rigors of field service and the lingering effects of his injury forced him to give up active service in November 1864. He held various non-combat commands until the end of the war. "Hancock the Superb" died in 1886 and was laid to rest at Montgomery Cemetery near his boyhood home of Norristown, Pennsylvania, in a mausoleum of his own design.

(LIBRARY OF CONGRESS)

MAJ. GEN. DANIEL EDGAR SICKLES
Commander, III Corps
(October 20, 1819 – May 3, 1914)

Perhaps no commander on either side evokes as much enduring controversy as Dan Sickles. On the second day of the battle, Sickles advanced without orders nearly his entire III Corps from its initial left flank position north of Little Round Top westward to the Emmitsburg Road. The move created a salient impossible to defend with the troops he possessed.

At Gettysburg on July 2, Maj. Gen. George G. Meade ordered Sickles to place his corps on the left flank of the defensive line, anchored on the right by Hancock's II Corps and on the left by Little Round Top. Dissatisfied with the position, Sickles marched his corps about one-half mile ahead to slightly higher ground along the Emmitsburg Road. Shortly after he reached this position Sickles' Corps was attacked on two sides by Lt. Gen. James Longstreet's Southern infantry and suffered heavy casualties. The fighting made famous such memorable terrain features as the Peach Orchard, Devil's Den, and the Valley of Death. One of the longest surviving Gettysburg generals, Sickles died in 1914 and was buried in Arlington Cemetery.

MAJ. GEN. GOUVERNEUR KEMBLE WARREN

Chief of Engineers, Army of the Potomac
(January 8, 1830 – August 8, 1882)

(LIBRARY OF CONGRESS)

Known today as "The Savior of Little Round Top," Warren's finest day was July 2 at Gettysburg.

That day, Warren realized the importance of the undefended Little Round Top to the rest of the Federal line. Without orders and without consulting his superiors, Warren ordered a brigade to occupy the hill only minutes before large numbers of Confederates attacked into the area. He suffered a minor wound to the neck during the action, his second injury of the war.

Warren's heroic likeness stands atop a boulder on Little Round Top, one of the most photographed and recognizable statues in the world. It is also one of the few monuments on the field funded entirely with private money, raised by his comrades, friends, and admirers.

MAJ. GEN. ALFRED PLEASONTON

Commander, Cavalry Corps
(July 7, 1824 – February 17, 1897)

(LIBRARY OF CONGRESS)

Pleasonton issued two key orders while in command of the Federal army's Cavalry Corps during the Gettysburg Campaign. One was obeyed and the other was not. Both critically impacted Gettysburg. The manner in which he deployed his cavalry following the battle may have played a role in allowing the Confederate army to escape across the Potomac River.

On the second day at Gettysburg Pleasonton ordered the bulk of the cavalry on the field at the time, two brigades under Brig. Gen. John Buford on the left flank, to ride miles away to rest and refit. One of the results of this decision left Maj. Gen. Daniel E. Sickles' III Corps on the left flank of the Federal line without a cavalry screen. Sickles moved most of his corps one-half mile forward, ahead of the rest of the line, and was attacked there and crushed during the Confederate assault late that afternoon.

On the following day (July 3) Pleasonton ordered the cavalry on the right flank, a division under Brig. Gen. David M. Gregg, to leave that sector and move toward the center of the line. Gregg refused. His division, along with a brigade of cavalry under Brig. Gen. George A. Custer, fought off an assault there by a Confederate cavalry division under Maj. Gen. J.E.B. Stuart about the same time Pickett's Charge was hitting Cemetery Ridge.

Pleasonton resigned his commission in 1868 and served in various government roles for twenty years. He died in his sleep in Washington, D.C. in 1897 and is buried in Congressional Cemetery.

BRIG. GEN. JOHN BUFORD
Commander, 1st Division, Cavalry Corps
(March 4, 1826 – December 16, 1863)

One of the Federal cavalry's most efficient and skilled officers, the pivotal moment of Buford's career came on the first day at Gettysburg. On the morning of July 1, 1863, two of his three brigades met and engaged advancing Confederate forces west of town. Buford's determination to defend the high ground led to the selection of Gettysburg as the field of battle between the armies.

He arrived in Gettysburg at the head of two brigades about midday on June 30, 1863. At that time General Lee's Army of Northern Virginia was west and north of town. The information Buford gathered on the location of the enemy convinced him that Gettysburg would be attacked the following day. He set up a perimeter of videttes (the cavalry's equivalent of infantry outposts) to watch the roads leading into the town. Early the next morning, July 1, one of Buford's troopers opened the historic battle when he fired a shot at Confederate infantry marching along the pike leading east from Cashtown to Gettysburg.

Buford's troopers conducted a slow fighting withdrawal that slowed down the Confederate infantry until Federal infantry from Reynolds' I Corps arrived on the field. Although much of the Union army that fought around Gettysburg that day was routed, by dusk on July 1 the Federals held good high ground southeast and south of town – terrain Buford had helped secure.

He continued leading his troopers in the campaigns in Virginia until December 1863, when he fell ill. He left the army and traveled to Washington, D.C., and died on December 16 of typhoid fever, and is buried at West Point Cemetery.

BRIG. GEN. DAVID McMURTRIE GREGG
Commander, 2nd Division, Cavalry Corps
(April 10, 1833 – August 7, 1916)

(LIBRARY OF CONGRESS)

David Gregg's accomplishments at Gettysburg are overshadowed by those of a subordinate, Brig. Gen. George A. Custer, who fought under Gregg on East Cavalry Field on July 3. Pickett's Charge was underway that afternoon when Gregg battled veteran Southern cavalry under Maj. Gen. J.E.B. Stuart about four miles farther east.

Gregg and his troopers arrived on the battlefield late on July 2 and took position on the right flank of the Army of the Potomac east of the main battlefield. Stuart determined to attack Gregg on that flank the next day. About midday on July 3, Stuart and Gregg began skirmishing along the fields of the nearby John Rummel farm as Pickett's Charge began. Two brigades of the 3rd Cavalry Division under Brig. Gen. Judson Kilpatrick were leaving for the army's opposite (left) flank. When he saw Brig. Gen. George A. Custer and his brigade arriving, Gregg asked Custer to remain with him instead on the far right to help against Stuart. Custer agreed, and under Gregg's direction Custer led a mounted assault with his Michigan cavalry troops that checked Stuart's advance. Gregg's efforts protected the Union right flank. When Pickett's Charge ended, Lee's Confederates had been repulsed at all points.

Gregg resigned his commission in late January 1865 and left the army. After trying life as a farmer in Reading, Pennsylvania, Gregg was appointed consul to Austria-Hungary by President Ulysses S. Grant in 1874. When he died in Reading in 1916, Gregg was one of the oldest surviving Pennsylvania veterans of the Civil War. He is buried in Charles Evans Cemetery. A nearby equestrian statue memorializes one of Reading's favorite sons.

(LIBRARY OF CONGRESS)

BRIG. GEN. ELON JOHN FARNSWORTH

Commander, 1st Brigade, 3rd Division, Cavalry Corps
(July 30, 1837 – July 3, 1863)

On July 3, twenty-five-year-old Brig. Gen. Elon Farnsworth led a mounted cavalry charge into the Confederate right flank just south of Devil's Den. Mortally wounded, he fell with many of his men just as Pickett's Charge to the north was being repulsed.

During the later stages of Pickett's Charge late on the afternoon of July 3, Farnsworth's division commander, Brig. Gen. H. Judson Kilpatrick, ordered him to lead a mounted cavalry charge over wooded and rocky terrain. Farnsworth believed the charge doomed to fail, but led his men valiantly through woods and around boulders into the rear of the Confederate line. Nearly surrounded, many of Farnsworth's men were killed or wounded and Farnsworth was shot several times. His body was discovered by his surviving comrades the next day.

One of the youngest generals in the Federal army, Farnsworth was the only one killed at Gettysburg leading a charge behind Rebel lines. He was first buried in Gettysburg's Evergreen Cemetery, and later moved to the Rockton Cemetery at Rockton, Illinois.

(LIBRARY OF CONGRESS)

COL. HARRISON HERBERT JEFFORDS

Commander, 4th Michigan Infantry
(August 21, 1834 – July 3, 1863)

On July 2, Jeffords and his men were marched into George Rose's wheatfield as the position was being attacked by Georgia Confederates. During hand-to-hand fighting a Southerner grabbed the 4th Michigan's colors as a prize. Jeffords shot the Rebel and took back the banner. He was immediately shot in the thigh. Moments later, a Confederate rushed forward and thrust his bayonet into Jeffords' stomach.

The Michigan colonel was carried to the rear to a field hospital, where he died early the next day. He is buried in Forest Lawn Cemetery in Dexter, Michigan, the highest-ranking officer during the Civil War known to have died from a bayonet wound. He is memorialized in a dramatic painting by artist Don Troiani called "Saving the Flag."

Color Sgt. Benjamin H. Crippen

143rd Pennsylvania Infantry
(c. 1842 – July 1, 1863)

(CAMPFIRES AND BATTLEFIELDS)

Mid-morning on July 1, 1863, the 143rd Pennsylvania Infantry prepared for its first significant combat. Sgt. Crippen carried the colors of his regiment and led his men into the early infantry fighting on the Edward McPherson farm west of Gettysburg. The fighting along the Chambersburg Pike grew especially desperate for the Federals when the 143rd Pennsylvania and other organizations were overrun by a strong Confederate attack and forced to retreat east to Seminary Ridge. Young Crippen, however, was the last to retreat. Periodically, the 6'1" tall sergeant would stop, turn, and shake his fist at his pursuers. His horrified comrades watched as enemy lead dropped him. Even Lt. Gen. Ambrose P. Hill, the commander of the Confederate Third Corps, was sorry to see the brave young man fall.

Crippen's body was left on the field behind Confederate lines for the remainder of the battle. It was never identified. He probably rests among nearly 1,000 unidentified Federal remains in the Soldiers' National Cemetery at Gettysburg. The 143rd Pennsylvania's monument, placed in 1889 near the spot where Crippen fell with his colors, features his life-size stone relief shaking a fist at a now imaginary wave of Confederates.

Pvt. Alfred G. Gardner

1st Rhode Island Light Artillery, Battery B
(Died July 3, 1863)

On the afternoon of July 3, Confederate artillery along Seminary Ridge hammered the Federal line along the stone wall on Cemetery Ridge in preparation for Pickett's Charge. Gunners of Battery B, 1st Rhode Island Light Artillery responded with many other batteries up and down the Federal line. Pvt. Alfred Gardner was placing another cannonball into a 12-pound smoothbore Napoleon when a Confederate shell struck the muzzle and exploded, killing one of his comrades and nearly tearing off Gardner's left arm. The mortally wounded private fell to the ground and shouted, "Glory to God! I am happy! Hallelujah!" He died a few minutes later.

The Confederate shot that killed him bent the muzzle of the gun and jammed Gardner's round in the top of the tube. His fellow gunners tried to finish loading the ball so it could be fired, and even pounded it with the flat of an axe, to no avail. Unable to be fired, the gun had to be retired to the rear.

Gardner was initially buried on the grounds of a Federal field hospital, and was later interred in the small Rhode Island section of the Soldiers' National Cemetery beside his fellow gunner killed by the same cannon shot. Gardner's fieldpiece, known today as "The Gettysburg Gun," stands as an exhibit in the Rhode Island State House in Providence. The cannon ball Gardner was attempting to load that afternoon of July 3, 1863, can still be seen wedged at the muzzle.

Confederate Officers and Soldiers

GEN. ROBERT EDWARD LEE
Commander, Army of Northern Virginia
(January 19, 1807 – October 12, 1870)

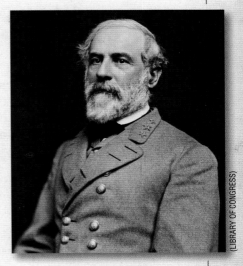

Despite his defeat at Gettysburg and the ultimate loss of the Civil War in the Eastern Theater, Robert E. Lee is considered by many historians to be one of America's most talented military officers.

During the march to Pennsylvania in June 1863, Lee hoped to meet and fall upon separate parts of the Federal Army of the Potomac and defeat each in detail. He did not expect the bulk of the Northern army to be close to Gettysburg when the main battle opened on July 1. His sweeping success that day drove Lee to resume the offensive on both the following days. Despite several near-misses, his army was repulsed at all points. After suffering heavy losses, including unusually high casualties among his officers, Lee had no choice but to retreat into Virginia. Gettysburg was the last major offensive operation launched by the Army of Northern Virginia.

Driven from Petersburg, Virginia in early April 1865, Lee surrendered one week later to Ulysses S. Grant at Appomattox Court House, effectively ending the Civil War. The grounds of his home, Arlington House, were turned into a cemetery for Federal soldiers, thus ensuring that Lee could never return to it again.

After the war Lee encouraged his former Confederates to reconcile with Northerners. In October 1865 he became president of Washington College (today Washington and Lee University) and began work on his memoirs. In September 1870, however, he suffered a stroke and died on October 12 of pneumonia. He reposes underneath the Lee Chapel at the university in Lexington, Virginia, which attracts thousands of visitors each year.

(LIBRARY OF CONGRESS)

LT. GEN. JAMES LONGSTREET
Commander, Longstreet's (First) Corps
(January 8, 1821 – January 2, 1904)

General Longstreet turned in his most controversial (and arguably his best) service of the war at Gettysburg on July 2, when his late-arriving hammer stroke caved in the Union left flank late that afternoon and opened other opportunities for attack up and down the long Union line of battle.

But Longstreet's Gettysburg performance has triggered heated debate. During the era of the "Lost Cause" following the war, Southern partisans tried to blame him for the Gettysburg defeat in an effort to shift blame away from General Lee. Longstreet was roundly criticized for being "too slow" and unwilling to fight aggressively at Gettysburg. Although there is some justification for his foot-dragging on July 2, once he attacked he struck hard, collapsing Sickles' line and nearly capturing Little Round Top. Longstreet was also blamed for not having sufficient confidence in Pickett's Charge on July 3. In his memoirs Longstreet criticized Lee's handling of the battle, which added to the vitriol heaped upon the former corps commander by proponents of the "Lost Cause."

Longstreet settled in New Orleans, Louisiana, with his family after the war. Embroiled in the "Lost Cause" controversy, he moved back to Georgia and held various government appointments. His memoirs *From Manassas to Appomattox* were published in 1896, eight years before his death from pneumonia. He is buried in Alta Vista Cemetery in Gainesville.

Lt. Gen. Richard Stoddert Ewell

Commander, Ewell's (Second) Corps
(February 8, 1817 – January 25, 1872)

(LIBRARY OF CONGRESS)

Like so many other high ranking officers, Second Corps commander Richard Ewell's Gettysburg performance is also the subject of much debate. After his men routed the Federal XI Corps north of town on the first day of the battle, General Lee gave Ewell the discretion to assault the Federals rallying atop Cemetery Hill if he deemed it "practicable" to do so. Ewell decided not to attack and Cemetery Hill and Cemetery Ridge to its south were turned into a bastion of defense Lee was unable to break over the course of two more days of battle.

During the early stages of the Gettysburg Campaign Ewell captured the Federal garrison at Winchester in Virginia and his corps was the first to enter Pennsylvania. His broad attack north of town on July 1 enveloped the Federal XI Corps and captured thousands of prisoners. After he decided not to attack Cemetery Hill late in the day, the Federals strengthened the high ground. Ewell's heavy assaults against Culp's Hill and East Cemetery Hill on July 2-3 were unsuccessful.

After the war Ewell retired to his wife Lizinka's farm in Tennessee, where he lived long enough to endure his share of public blame for the loss at Gettysburg. He and Lizinka died three days apart of pneumonia in 1872, and are buried in the Old City Cemetery at Nashville.

Lt. Gen. Ambrose Powell Hill

Commander, Hill's (Third) Corps
(November 9, 1825 – April 2, 1865)

Historians have a difficult time relating General Hill's role at Gettysburg because we know so little about it. "Little Powell," as he was known to his men, suffered from ill health for much of his adult life, a condition that often worsened significantly during times of high stress.

(LIBRARY OF CONGRESS)

163

He led his Third Corps during the advance into Pennsylvania in June 1863, but was weakened by illness as the Battle of Gettysburg began on July 1. There are very few contemporary references to Hill on the field during the battle, and he seems to have taken little active part in the command of his corps.

On April 2, 1865, just one week before Lee surrendered at Appomattox, Hill was shot and killed by a Federal soldier while riding along the Petersburg front. Hill was buried in a private cemetery in Chesterfield, and his remains were re-interred in Richmond's Hollywood Cemetery two years later. In 1892, Hill was reburied under his massive equestrian monument along what is now a busy and noisy street in Richmond.

MAJ. GEN. GEORGE EDWARD PICKETT
Commander, Pickett's Division, Longstreet's Corps
(January 16, 1825 – July 30, 1875)

George Pickett will forever be remembered for the failed July 3 infantry charge at Gettysburg that bears his name (although two other divisions participated and Pickett was not in command of all the troops in the charge). He mourned for the rest of his life the destruction of his division. After the war Pickett met Gen. Robert E. Lee, the Confederate commander who ordered the charge. According to an eyewitness, Pickett later told him, "That man destroyed my division."

Pickett and his division arrived on the Gettysburg battlefield late on July 2. The following day General Lee formulated his plan for a massive infantry assault against the center of the Union line along Cemetery Ridge. The assaulting force was composed of Pickett's fresh division and two others from Hill's Third Corps with brigades already bloodied from earlier fighting. Pickett's command suffered more than 50% casualties. Every brigade and regimental commander was either killed, wounded, and/or captured. When Lee implored Pickett to ready his men for a possible Federal counterassault, Pickett reportedly told his commander, "General Lee, I have no division now."

Following Gettysburg, Pickett served in commands outside the Army of Northern Virginia and returned to what remained of his division in 1864 for the Overland Campaign. Pickett's defeat at Five Forks on April 1, 1865, unhinged the right flank of the Confederate army and hastened the collapse of the Petersburg defenses. Pickett surrendered with his division at Appomattox Court House on April 9 but he fled to Canada with his young wife because he was afraid of being prosecuted for treason. They returned to Virginia in 1866. Pickett sold insurance for the New York Life Insurance Company and died in 1875 of scarlet fever. His grave at Richmond's Hollywood Cemetery, marked with an elaborate stone memorial placed in 1875, is visited often by tourists.

Lt. Col. Benjamin Franklin Carter

Commander, 4th Texas Infantry
(1831 – July 21, 1863)

(J. DAVID PETRUZZI)

Carter's Gettysburg saga is one of the more interesting and tragic tales of a battle rife with them. Mortally wounded on July 2, his remains lay in an unmarked Pennsylvania grave for 147 years until it was discovered and properly marked with a new headstone in 2010.

During Longstreet's assault on July 2 against the Union left, Carter fell mortally wounded on the western face of Little Round Top. Carter was carried off the field and taken along when the Confederate army retreated on July 5. When the wagon ride proved too painful and strenuous, he was left at a home south of Gettysburg. Captured by Federals, Carter was taken to Chambersburg, Pennsylvania, with many other captured and wounded Southerners. At the Academy Hospital in Chambersburg, Carter died on July 21.

When it proved difficult to find a place that would accept a Rebel officer's remains, he was interred in the cemetery of the town's Methodist Church. His grave was either inadequately marked or was not marked at all. In 1896 the cemetery's occupants were moved to the town's Cedar Grove Cemetery, where Carter's unidentified remains rested in yet another unknown grave. After years of research, a group of historians (including author J. David Petruzzi) located Carter's grave in 2009 and a proper headstone with Southern honors was erected the following year.

(LIBRARY OF CONGRESS)

PVT. JOHN WESLEY CULP

2nd Virginia Infantry
(1839 – July 2, 1863)

Born near Gettysburg, Wesley Culp likely played and hunted in the woods of Culp's Hill, an area owned by a relative named Henry Culp. In 1856 Wesley relocated to Shepherdstown, Virginia, to work as a carriage maker. When the Civil War began, he enlisted in a Virginia infantry unit. On July 2 Wesley was fighting on his regiment's skirmish line at the Christian Benner farm, a parcel of land adjoining Henry Culp's land. Wesley was killed that morning and eventually buried on the battlefield in an unmarked or poorly marked grave. Later attempts to identify his resting place proved unsuccessful.

Several legends surround his burial. According to one story, his family found his body and buried it in the town's Evergreen Cemetery. It is likely that Culp was exhumed with his comrades and reentered in a mass unknown grave (perhaps with other Gettysburg unknowns in Hollywood Cemetery in Richmond, Virginia). Or, he may still repose in sight of his relative's land on the battlefield. Either way, it was a tragic "homecoming" for one of Gettysburg's native sons.

Battlefield Photographers

(LIBRARY OF CONGRESS)

MATHEW BRADY

(May 18, 1823/24 – January 15, 1896)

Today Brady is the most recognized and appreciated of the 19th century American photographers, almost exclusively because of voluminous record of the Civil War. Brady and his assistants produced more than 10,000 photographic plates during his lifetime, a priceless visual history of the period.

Brady opened a studio in Washington, D.C. in 1847 and began taking pictures of government leaders. Brady's work received much praise but, ironically, his eyesight began to fail at a relatively young age. The man most famous for bringing history to the world through the eyes of a camera would soon be all but blind.

Brady saw the special opportunity the Civil War offered a photographer. With nearly two dozen assistants (among them Timothy O'Sullivan and Alexander Gardner), each traveling with their own darkroom wagon, Brady set out to photograph the conflict. Brady's photographs of the dead at Antietam shocked America and the world; it was the first time the public had seen photographs of dead bodies on a battlefield. Besides Antietam, Brady's most famous battlefield photography was captured at Gettysburg. Because of his poor eyesight, Brady took few photographs himself, leaving the task to his teams of photographers.

The public was tired of the carnage and after the war had little interest in Brady's photographs. Brady hoped the government would purchase them, but when it refused he went bankrupt. His wife died in 1887, and by that time he was depressed and financially ruined. Brady died in the charity ward of Presbyterian Hospital, penniless and unappreciated. Veterans of the 7th New York Infantry paid for his funeral and his interment in Washington's Congressional Cemetery.

Although thousands of his glass negatives were lost or destroyed, thousands more reside in the Library of Congress and the National Archives. Each of them is a priceless record of American history.

ALEXANDER GARDNER
(October 17, 1821 – December 10, 1882)

A former employee of Mathew Brady's gallery, Alexander Gardner was one of Brady's main competitors of Civil War photography. Like Brady, Gardner's photography rose to prominence with images from the battles of Antietam and Gettysburg. Gardner is also remembered for the last photographs of President Lincoln ever taken, as well as those of the hanging of the Lincoln assassination conspirators.

After the start of the war when Gardner became

Federal army commander Maj. Gen. George B. McClellan's staff photographer, he soon resigned from Brady's operation. Gardner took many images of the Antietam battlefield in September 1862 as well as at Fredericksburg during the winter of 1862. In May 1863 he opened his own studio in Washington, D.C. with his brother James, hiring away many of Brady's employees in the process. Gardner and his team, including Timothy O'Sullivan and James F. Gibson, took many photographs of the Gettysburg battlefield. Perhaps his most famous image is the staged "Rebel Sharpshooter" in Devil's Den.

In 1866 Gardner published a two-volume work of many of his wartime photographs. He later left the photography business to establish an insurance company in Washington, D.C., which he managed until his death. He is buried in Glenwood Cemetery in Washington, D.C.

TIMOTHY H. O'SULLIVAN
(c. 1840 – January 14, 1882)

(LIBRARY OF CONGRESS)

Timothy O'Sullivan is the least known of Civil War photographers. Like Alexander Gardner, O'Sullivan also worked for Mathew Brady's studio before the war before joining Gardner's studio. He helped create many of the famous Gardner photographs of Gettysburg.

At the start of the Civil War, O'Sullivan was a civilian attached to the Federal army and photographed operations in Virginia, the Carolinas, and Georgia until the summer of 1862. Thereafter he left Brady's studio with Gardner, joining the latter's own studio and team of photographers. O'Sullivan worked closely with Gardner at Gettysburg only days after the battle, assisting with the creation of many of the battlefield's most famous images. He remained with Gardner until the end of the war and created with him many of the lasting images of the final year, including images from the siege of Petersburg and the Appomattox Campaign.

For several years following the war O'Sullivan was the government's official photographer. He continued to work for the government until falling gravely ill with tuberculosis, which eventually claimed his life. He died in Washington and is buried in St. Peter's Cemetery in West New Brighton, New York.

Gettysburg Civilians

MATILDA "TILLIE" PIERCE ALLEMAN
(March 11, 1848 – March 15, 1914)

Fifteen-year-old Tillie Pierce lived with her family on Baltimore Street when the battle began. Thinking it would be safer, she relocated with some friends outside town at a farm near Little Round Top. That area, however, soon became part of the Federal battle line and a focus of the Confederate attacks of July 2. Tillie brought water and food to the soldiers, and helped medical personnel care for the wounded. On July 7, after the Confederate army left the field, she ventured back to her home and was astonished at the devastation. She continued to care for the wounded and dying, and in 1889 published an account of her experiences. Her book, *At Gettysburg: Or What a Girl Saw and Heard at the Battle,* is a well-known and useful account of the civilian experience. She married Horace Alleman and they moved to Selinsgrove, Pennsylvania, where she is buried in Trinity Lutheran Cemetery.

DAVID McCONAUGHY
(July 13, 1823 – January 14, 1902)

Well-known Gettysburg attorney David McConaughy was active in the war nearly as soon as it began. In 1861, he led a group of his clients to form a company of home guard scouts. During the Gettysburg Campaign McConaughy constantly furnished intelligence on Confederate movements to the state government as well as Federal troops.

He and his scouts sent information to Harrisburg about all nearby Confederate movements during the first two years of the war. The group was particularly active in late June 1863 when various Southern units moved throughout the Gettysburg area. Shortly after the battle, McConaughy began purchasing battlefield land to preserve it. His desire was to establish a national cemetery for the Federal dead (the initial location he chose was the area of the present-day Pennsylvania Monument). His efforts, and subsequent recognition thereof, are overshadowed by those of rival Gettysburg attorney David Wills, who was ultimately appointed to oversee the creation of the Soldier's National Cemetery. All but unknown to most casual students of Gettysburg, McConaughy deserves a great deal of credit for the preservation of battlefield land, as well as the creation of the Gettysburg Battlefield Memorial Association (the first group responsible for preservation of, and monument placement on, the field). He is buried in the town's Evergreen Cemetery, the burial ground he helped to establish in the 1850's.

(LIBRARY OF CONGRESS)

ELIZABETH SALOME "SALLIE" MYERS STEWART
(June 24, 1842 – January 17, 1922)

Sallie was a twenty-one-year-old schoolteacher when the war came to Gettysburg in July 1863. After spending much of the first day of the battle in the basement of her Baltimore Street home with her family, she emerged to nurse wounded soldiers at St. Francis Xavier Catholic Church the following day. One of the soldiers she cared for was mortally wounded Sgt. Alexander Stewart of the 149th Pennsylvania Infantry. His condition made Sallie cry, but she stayed by his side. When Stewart died on July 6, Sallie contacted his family with the sad news.

The following year, Stewart's widow and his younger brother Henry visited Sallie to thank her for caring for their soldier. Sallie and Henry Stewart began courting and married in 1867. Sadly, Henry died the following year from complications of his own war wound while Sallie was pregnant. Their son, Henry Alexander Stewart, grew up to be a well-known and beloved Gettysburg physician. In honor of his father and uncle, as well as the service of his mother's care for wounded soldiers, Dr. Stewart made sure a flag decorated the grave of every deceased soldier in Adams County on Memorial Day each year. Sallie is buried in Gettysburg's Evergreen Cemetery.

ELIZABETH THORN
(December 28, 1832 – October 17, 1907)

Elizabeth Thorn's experience during the battle is a story of fortitude and determination. Interim caretaker of the town's Evergreen Cemetery while her caretaker husband Peter fought in the Federal army, Elizabeth assisted in the burial of nearly 100 casualties of the battle, all while she was six months pregnant.

During the Battle of Gettysburg, Peter was serving at Harpers Ferry in West Virginia. Since Elizabeth's home, which was also the Evergreen Cemetery Gatehouse (today a famous battlefield fixture) sat right in the center of the Federal battle line, the fighting swirled around her for all three days. After the battle, and with very little assistance, the pregnant Elizabeth conducted dozens of burials of Federal dead, which were later moved to the Soldiers' National Cemetery when it was established later that year. She is buried with her husband Peter in Evergreen, resting in the soil in which she worked so hard in the days following the horrific battle.

(LIBRARY OF CONGRESS)

MARY VIRGINIA "JENNIE" WADE
(May 21, 1843 – July 3, 1863)

The only civilian killed during the three-day battle, Jennie (her family actually called her "Ginnie") is today the most well-known town resident of the time. While preparing bread dough in her sister's Baltimore Street home on the morning of July 3, a stray bullet crashed through two doors and struck Jennie in the back, killing her instantly.

When Confederates occupied most of the town on July 1, she left her Breckenridge Street home and went to her sister's home, closer to the Federal lines. No one knows who pulled the trigger that sent the fateful bullet on its tragic course. Perhaps it was meant for a soldier in blue on nearby Cemetery Hill, but it killed an innocent twenty-year-old girl.

(LIBRARY OF CONGRESS)

171

Jennie was first buried in the garden behind the home. In January 1864 she was re-buried in a church cemetery along Stratton Street. Finally, in November 1865, Jennie was finally laid to rest in the town's Evergreen Cemetery, where her grave is today the most sought-after burial site. The monument marking her grave was installed in 1900, and under a special government provision, a flag flies day and night over her gravesite.

(LIBRARY OF CONGRESS)

DAVID WILLS

(February 3, 1831 – October 27, 1894)

Gettysburg attorney David Wills is best known as the citizen who invited President Abraham Lincoln to speak at the dedication of the Soldiers' National Cemetery in November, 1863. Wills hosted the president in his home the night before Lincoln's address, a short but brilliant speech that has become one of the most important in American history.

After the battle, Wills was appointed by the state to supervise the creation of the Soldiers' National Cemetery. Several nationally-known figures were invited to attend. Almost as an afterthought Wills invited President Lincoln to come and give "a few appropriate remarks."

Wills is buried with several members of his family in Gettysburg's Evergreen Cemetery. His home (which also houses his law office and the bedroom in which Lincoln stayed) still stands on Gettysburg's town square and hosts thousands of visitors each year.

Visiting Gettysburg

 It is estimated that as many as two million people visit **Gettysburg** each year. Visitors range from the casually curious to the diehard students of the battle. Regardless of your level of interest or knowledge, what is the best way to visit Gettysburg? How should you begin to plan your visit? If your time is limited, what must-see sights and spots on the battlefield and in town do you need to see before you leave? This section will help answer these questions and provide additional resources to get you started.

The Internet is a wonderful planning tool, so we suggest you visit some of the websites in the next section "Gettysburg on the Internet" to get some background information and a good feel for what is available. We especially recommend the pages of the **National Park Service**, the **Gettysburg Museum and Visitor Center**, the **Association of Gettysburg Licensed Battlefield Guides**, and the **Association of Gettysburg Licensed Town Guides**. These websites provide you with contact information to make your visit much more enjoyable and rewarding. The Battlefield Guides and Town Guides offer custom tours tailored to exactly what you want to see, whether it is the entire battlefield, just the town, or specific areas and actions that are of interest to you. During the anniversary of the battle each year (July 1, 2, and 3) and on other select days before and after, the knowledgeable park rangers at Gettysburg conduct free "battle walks" that are educational and enjoyable. You will find this information on the National Park Service's website.

If you want to read more on your own before or during your visit, and have something to take out to the field in addition to the book you are now reading, consider acquiring a copy of *The Complete Gettysburg Guide* (Savas Beatie, 2009), which features tours of the main battlefield, the surrounding battlefields such as Hunterstown, Fairfield, and East Cavalry Field, field hospital sights, Evergreen Cemetery, the Soldiers' National Cemetery, and even rock carvings found around the field. The full-color guide includes nearly 70 original maps that you can use while self-touring or in conjunction with tours led by rangers and Licensed Guides. The book can be purchased online, at most bookstores in Gettysburg (including at the Museum and Visitor Center), from the publisher, and signed copies from the authors' website at **www.completegettysburgguide.com**.

The best place to begin at Gettysburg is at the **Gettysburg Museum and Visitor Center**. This state-of-the-art facility, located at 1195 Baltimore Pike, boasts a fascinating museum that tells the story of the battle and this period of our nation's history. Not to be missed is the giant refurbished **Cyclorama painting**, completed in 1883 by artist Paul Phillippoteaux, which features the climax of Pickett's Charge on July 3, 1863. You will stand in the center of this 359-foot long cylindrical painting and behold a light and sound show that offers an exceptional "you are there" experience. Park rangers can be consulted in the museum and Licensed Guides can also be hired there. Maps (such as the Auto Tour of the battlefield) are available at the main counter. If you enjoy audio tours, we suggest *The Complete Gettysburg Guide Audio Tour*, which can be found in the Visitor Center that also includes a well-stocked book and gift store.

Once you have finished the educational experience of the Museum and Visitor Center, it is time to get out onto the battlefield! But where do you start? If you are self-touring and have a copy of *The Complete Gettysburg Guide*, a variety of choices are set forth for you to choose from. If your time is limited to only a few hours, following *The Complete Gettysburg Guide Audio Tour* or the Park Service's Auto Tour may be a good choice. Both will guide you to the battlefield of July 1 (the first day) and then to the fields and prominent sights and actions of July 2 and 3.

Must See Places

Visiting the huge sprawling battlefield can be a bit overwhelming the first time. One of the common questions asked by first-time visitors is "What are the 'must-see' areas of the battlefield and town?" Here are a few suggestions:

DAY ONE (JULY 1):

McPherson's Ridge: This general area west of town along the Chambersburg Pike is where Federal infantry from Reynolds' I Corps began fighting approaching Confederates on the morning of July 1. It was here the fighting escalated into a full battle.

Railroad Cut: This stunning feature, just north of the Chambersburg Pike on the first day's field, is where hundreds of Confederate soldiers were trapped and killed, wounded, and captured, in an exceptionally bloody and unexpected fight.

Oak Hill (and the Eternal Peace Light Memorial): This major elevation, about one-half mile north of the Railroad Cut, provides a wonderful view of the first day's battlefield, the town of Gettysburg, and Barlow's (Blocher's) Knoll. A division of Confederate infantry arrived on this hill, which also happened to be on the right flank of the Federals fighting the Southerners attacking from the west. Once you are on this height, you will immediately realize its significance to the battle.

Because of the manner in which the fight was conducted, you have to drive along Seminary Ridge to reach the jump-off point for the later July 2 afternoon battle on the southern end of the field. Along the way you will experience some wonderful views of the July 3 fighting before seeing sites associated with July 2.

When you finish on the first day's field, drive to Confederate Avenue along Seminary Ridge, where much of Robert E. Lee's Confederate army aligned itself for battle on July 2 and July 3. (Your Auto Tour or guidebook will show you where this is located.)

DAYS TWO AND THREE (JULY 2 AND 3):

Virginia Memorial: The area around the mammoth Virginia Memorial, topped with the statue of Lee upon his faithful horse Traveller, offers the same outstanding view of the field across which Pickett's Charge was launched that Lee himself enjoyed, as well as a good view of the Federal position on Cemetery Ridge about one mile to the east. Most of the Confederate memorials and monuments on the battlefield line Seminary Ridge. Take some time and examine some of them.

From the memorial, drive approximately one mile to reach an observation tower on the left side of the park road.

Longstreet's Tower: Climbing this observation tower is well worth the effort. The view offers a stunning vista of the fields, roads, and terrain across which Lt. Gen. James Longstreet's men attacked late on the afternoon of July 2. Ahead is the Peach Orchard, Rose Farm, and in the eastern distance Devil's Den and Little Round Top and Big Round Top. Look north and northeast while in the tower and you will get another view of the fields across which Pickett's Charge swept.

From the tower, drive approximately 1.7 miles to reach the summit of Little Round Top.

Little Round Top: If you take the time to visit Gettysburg, soaking in the breathtaking views from the summit of Little Round Top is a must. In addition to its famous monuments (among them the statue of Gouverneur K. Warren), the rocky hill provides a vista overlooking much of the Federal line to the north, nearly the entirety of the July 2 and 3 battlefield, the Confederate line to the west, and the South Mountain range many miles beyond. Below and to the west are the impressive boulders of Devil's Den, the massive stone witnesses to the fighting and dying of July 2. Today, the tumbling stones offer visiting children and adults a place to climb, play, explore, and ponder.

Drive approximately 1.5 miles north along the Federal line on Cemetery Ridge, where you will visit another necessary stop: the High Water Mark.

High Water Mark: On Cemetery Ridge directly opposite the Virginia Memorial is the stone wall where perhaps a few hundred Confederate infantry led by Brig. Gen. Lewis Armistead established what some refer to as the "High Water Mark of the Confederacy" at the height of Pickett's Charge. Waiting for them on the ridge were thousands of Federals and batteries of artillery. Also here is the famous "Copse of Trees," a battlefield landmark that, decades after the war, became a symbol of the deepest point of penetration. Also here is the famous "Bloody Angle," where the stone wall takes a turn to the east and was the scene of so much bloody carnage during the July 3 assault.

CULP'S HILL (JULY 2 AND 3):

If time allows, visit the anchor of the right flank of the Federal line at **Culp's Hill**. Like its sister hill Little Round Top on the Federal left flank a few miles to the south, Culp's Hill was the scene of extensive fighting and bloodshed on the afternoon and evening of July 2 and on the morning of July 3. On a clear day, the observation tower on the summit affords a wonderful view of much of the battlefield and its many landmarks.

THE TOWN OF GETTYSBURG:

Within the borough of Gettysburg, most of which also doubled as part of the battlefield in early July 1863, are many historic buildings and interesting things to see. Begin a town tour in the **town square** (called "The Diamond" in 1863 and "Lincoln Square" today). The large well-maintained building at the corner of the square and Rt. 30 East (York Street) is the **historic home and law offices of David Wills.** Wills invited President Abraham Lincoln to the dedication of the Soldiers' National Cemetery (at which the president gave the famous Gettysburg Address), and it was in this home that Lincoln spent the night before the event. The home is owned by the National Park Service and is an outstanding museum.

In addition to serving as hospitals during and after the battle, many historic churches with unique histories are sprinkled throughout town. Nearly every period home and structure in Gettysburg served as a hospital or as a refuge for soldiers of both sides. Any building that has a small "1863" plaque on the front is officially recognized as having stood during the battle. Throughout the town are waist-level waysides that describe a noteworthy action or event that took place on or near that spot.

Other structures of note worth a visit include the **Matilda "Tillie" Pierce home** (303 Baltimore Street); The **"Jennie" Wade House** (548 Baltimore Street, where she was killed by a bullet on July 3 while visiting her sister); the **Harvey Sweney House** (now known as the Farnsworth House at 401 Baltimore Street); the **George Shriver House** (309 Baltimore Street); and Gettysburg's oldest home, the **1776 Dobbin House** (89 Steinwehr Avenue).

Gettysburg on the Web

A search with just the word "Gettysburg" on the Internet turns up hundreds of thousands of web hits. Some websites are more useful and reliable than others. Many or even most contain questionable or inaccurate information. Below are the URLs of what we consider to be the best websites for planning a visit to Gettysburg and for learning more in terms of the Civil War in general, and specifically the armies and the officers and men who fought here. Many of these websites will lead you to others that will enable you to further indulge your interest. Happy searching.

GETTYSBURG INFORMATION

Gettysburg National Military Park (National Park Service)

www.nps.gov/gett

Gettysburg Foundation (Museum and Visitor Center)

www.gettysburgfoundation.org

Gettysburg Association of Licensed Battlefield Guides

www.gettysburgtourguides.org

Gettysburg Licensed Town Guides

www.gettysburgpa.org/guidedtour.htm

Gettysburg Monuments

www.gettysburg.stonesentinels.com

Gettysburg Virtual Tour

www.virtualgettysburg.com

Gettysburg History, Videos, and News

www.gettysburgdaily.com

Adams County, Pennsylvania

www.adamscounty.us

GETTYSBURG TRIP PLANNING

www.gettysbg.com

www.gettysburgbattlefieldtours.com

www.gettysburg.national-park.com

GETTYSBURG DISCUSSION FORUMS

www.militaryhistoryonline.com/forums

www.cwdgonline.org

www.civilwartalk.com/forums

Gettysburg Bookshelf

By no means comprehensive, this list will provide readers (serious Gettysburg buffs are likely already familiar with these titles) with a number of ideas for additional reading on a variety of campaign subjects. If you have an interest in building a balanced Gettysburg collection, this list is a good way to begin. Many of the older titles have been reprinted and are still available, and several are also available online.

GENERAL CAMPAIGN HISTORIES

Coddington, Edwin B. – *The Gettysburg Campaign: A Study in Command* (1968)

Hoke, Jacob – *The Great Invasion of 1863* (1887)

Nofi, Albert A. – *The Gettysburg Campaign: June-July 1863* (1986)

Sears, Stephen W. – *Gettysburg* (2003)

Stackpole, Edward J. – *They Met at Gettysburg* (1956)

Trudeau, Noah Andre – *Gettysburg: A Testing of Courage* (2002)

Tucker, Glenn – *High Tide at Gettysburg: The Campaign in Pennsylvania* (1958)

CAMPAIGN PRIOR TO THE BATTLE

Downey, Fairfax – *Clash of Cavalry: The Battle of Brandy Station* (1959)

Gottfried, Bradley M. – *Roads to Gettysburg: Lee's Invasion of the North, 1863* (2001)

McKinney, Joseph W. – *Brandy Station, Virginia, June 9, 1863: The Largest Cavalry Battle of the Civil War* (2006)

Mingus, Sr., Scott L. – *Flames Beyond Gettysburg: The Confederate Expedition to the Susquehanna River, June 1863* (2011)

Nye, Wilburg Sturtevant – *Here Come the Rebels!* (1965)

O'Neill, Jr., Robert F. – *The Cavalry Battles of Aldie, Middleburg and Upperville, June 10-27, 1863* (1993)

Schildt, John W. – *Roads to Gettysburg* (1978)

Wittenberg, Eric J. – *The Battle of Brandy Station: North America's Largest Cavalry Battle* (2010)

Wittenberg, Eric J. and J. David Petruzzi – *Plenty of Blame to Go Around: Jeb Stuart's Controversial Ride to Gettysburg* (2006)

JULY 1 – FIRST DAY OF THE BATTLE

Hassler, Jr., Warren W. – *Crisis at the Crossroads: The First Day at Gettysburg* (1970)

Martin, David G. – *Gettysburg: July 1 (Rev. Ed.)* (1996)

Pfanz, Harry W. – *Gettysburg: The First Day* (2001)

Shue, Richard S. – *Morning at Willoughby Run: The Opening Battle at Gettysburg, July 1, 1863* (1998)

JULY 2 – SECOND DAY OF THE BATTLE

Imhof, John – *Gettysburg Day Two: A Study in Maps* (1997)

Pfanz, Harry W. – *Gettysburg: The Second Day* (1987)

JULY 3 – THIRD DAY OF THE BATTLE

Gallagher, Gary W., ed. – *The Third Day at Gettysburg & Beyond* (1994)

Wert, Jeffry D. – *Gettysburg: Day Three* (2001)

RETREAT FROM GETTYSBURG

Brown, Kent Masterson – *Retreat From Gettysburg: Lee, Logistics & the Pennsylvania Campaign* (2005)

Schildt, John W. – *Roads From Gettysburg* (1979)

Wittenberg, Eric J., J. David Petruzzi, and Michael F. Nugent – *One Continuous Fight: The Retreat from Gettysburg and the Pursuit of Lee's Army of Northern Virginia, July 4-14, 1863* (2008)

AFTERMATH OF THE BATTLE ON THE GETTYSBURG AREA

Coco, Gregory A. – *A Strange and Blighted Land: Gettysburg – The Aftermath of a Battle* (1995)

Coco, Gregory A. – *A Vast Sea of Misery: A History and Guide to the Union and Confederate Hospitals at Gettysburg, July 1 – November 20, 1863* (1988)

Dreese, Michael A. – *The Hospital on Seminary Ridge at the Battle of Gettysburg* (2002)

Patterson, Gerard A. – *Debris of Battle: The Wounded of Gettysburg* (1997)

GETTYSBURG CIVILIANS

Alleman, Tillie (Pierce) – *At Gettysburg, or What a Girl Saw and Heard of the Battle* (1889)

Bennett, Gerald R. – *Days of Uncertainty and Dread: The Ordeal Endured by the Citizens at Gettysburg* (1994)

Skelly, Daniel Alexander – *A Boy's Experiences During the Battles of Gettysburg* (1932)

Slade, Jim and John Alexander – *Firestorm at Gettysburg: Civilian Voices, June – November 1863* (1998)

GETTYSBURG GENERALS

Tagg, Larry – *The Generals of Gettysburg: The Leaders of America's Greatest Battle* (1998)

GETTYSBURG MAP STUDIES

Gottfried, Bradley M. – *The Maps of Gettysburg: An Atlas of the Gettysburg Campaign, June 3 – July 13, 1863* (2007)

Laino, Philip – *Gettysburg Campaign Atlas* (2009)

GETTYSBURG CASUALTY STUDIES

Busey, John W. – *The Last Full Measure: Burials in the Soldiers' National Cemetery at Gettysburg* (1988)

Busey, John W. – *These Honored Dead: The Union Casualties at Gettysburg* (1996)

Kowalis, Jeffrey J. and Loree L. – *Died at Gettysburg! Illustrated Biographies of the Union Casualties at Gettysburg* (1998)

GETTYSBURG ARMIES STRENGTH AND LOSSES STUDIES

Busey, John W. and David G. Martin – *Regimental Strengths and Losses at Gettysburg 4th ed.* (2005)

Petruzzi, J. David and Steven Stanley – *The Gettysburg Campaign in Numbers and Losses: Synposes, Orders of Battle, Strengths, Casualties, and Maps, June 9 - July 14, 1863* (2011)

GETTYSBURG STATISTICS COMPILATIONS

Teague, Charles – *Gettysburg by the Numbers: The Essential Pocket Compendium of Crucial and Curious Data About the Battle* (2006)

GETTYSBURG PHOTOGRAPHIC STUDIES

Frassanito, William – *Gettysburg: A Journey in Time* (1975)

Frassanito, William – *Early Photography at Gettysburg* (1995)

Salmon, John S. – *Historic Photos of Gettysburg* (2007)

GETTYSBURG BATTLEFIELD TOUR GUIDES

Grimsley, Mark and Brooks D. Simpson – *Gettysburg: A Battlefield Guide* (1999)

Petruzzi, J. David and Steven Stanley – *The Complete Gettysburg Guide: Walking and Driving Tours of the Battlefield, Town, Cemeteries, Field Hospital Sites, and other Topics of Historical Interest* (2009)

GETTYSBURG HISTORICAL-BASED NOVELS

Meredith, Frank – *The Unfinished Work* (2010)

Shaara, Michael – *Killer Angels* (1974)

Williams, William G. – *Days of Darkness: The Gettysburg Civilians* (1986)

Williams, William G. – *That Vast Procession of Misery:*
Lee's Wounded Retreat from Gettysburg (2010)

GETTYSBURG ARTILLERY STUDIES

Coco, Gregory A. – *A Concise Guide to the Artillery at Gettysburg* (2007)

Cole, Phillip M. – *Civil War Artillery at Gettysburg:*
Organization, Equipment, Ammunition, and Tactics (2002)

Newton, George W. – *Silent Sentinels: A Reference Guide to the Artillery at Gettysburg* (2005)

Spruill, Matt – *Summer Thunder: A Battlefield Guide to the Artillery at Gettysburg* (2010)

GETTYSBURG CAVALRY STUDIES

Longacre, Edward G. – *The Cavalry at Gettysburg: A Tactical Study of Mounted Operations*
during the Civil War's Pivotal Campaign, 9 June – 14 July 1863 (1986)

Wittenberg, Eric J. – *Gettysburg's Forgotten Cavalry Actions* (Rev. Ed. 2011)

Wittenberg, Eric J. – *Protecting the Flank: The Battles for*
Brinkerhoff's Ridge and East Cavalry Field (Rev. Ed. 2011)

GETTYSBURG MONUMENTS

Harrison, Kathy Georg, comp. – *The Location of the Monuments, Markers,*
and Tablets on Gettysburg Battlefield (1993)

Hartwig, D. Scott and Ann Marie – *Gettysburg: The Complete*
Pictorial of Battlefield Monuments (1988)

Hawthorne, Frederick W. – *Gettysburg: Stories of Men*
and Monuments as Told by Battlefield Guides (1988)

Martin, David G. – *Confederate Monuments at Gettysburg* (1995)